NOTHING TO LOSE

MOMENTS OF CONVICTION THAT CHANGED MY LIFE

Edir Macedo

NOTHING TO LOSE

MOMENTS OF CONVICTION THAT CHANGED MY LIFE

Translation
Derek Sevante

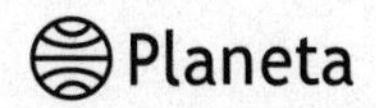
Planeta

Obra editada en colaboración con Editora Planeta do Brasil Ltda - Brasil

Título original: *Nada a perder – Momentos de convicção que mudaram a minha vida*

Revisión y corrección de estilo: Pablo Moronta
Revisión de prueba: Fernando C. Moura
Diagramación: Mauro C. Naxara
Fotografías de interiores: Archivo Diário SP, Lumi Zúnica, Evelson de Freitas/AE, Demetrio Koch, José Célio, Pauty Araújo, archivo personal, Reproducción TV Record y CEDOC/Unipro
Portada: Morais
Imagen de portada: Demetrio Koch

Colaboración: Karla Dunder, Marcus Souza, Anne Campos, Isney Savoy, Vagner Silva y Leandro Cipoloni
Agradecimientos: Cristiane Cardoso, Renato Cardoso, Edna Macedo, Marcus Vinicius Vieira, Clodomir Santos, Romualdo Panceiro, Celso Junior, Guaracy Santos, Honorilton Gonçalves, Marcos Pereira, Luiz Moraes, Adriana Guerra, Rita Cruz, Terezinha Rosa Silva, Mariléa Sales, Alba Maria, Albino da Silva y Sheila Tavolaro

Bajo el sello editorial PLANETA M.R.
Avenida Presidente Masarik núm. 111, 2o. piso
Colonia Chapultepec Morales
C.P. 11570, México, D.F.
www.editorialplaneta.com.mx

Primera edición impresa en México: enero de 2013
ISBN: 978-607-07-1494-8

Impreso en los talleres de Litográfica Ingramex, S.A. de C.V.
Centeno núm. 162, colonia Granjas Esmeralda, México, D.F.
Impreso en México – *Printed in Mexico*

CONTENTS

To my God, the Lord of my life.
Nothing that happened would have been possible without God's Spirit.

Introduction

We have two ways of looking at the past. Recall the moments we've lived through, feel the pain from wounds that still linger, and become a slave to these hard, painful memories. The other option is to learn from the past and bring those truths into the present, turning them into learning experiences—making use of faith in the Bible to understand that suffering produces perseverance; perseverance, character; and character, hope. (Romans 5:3-4)

God inspired Moses the prophet to spur the memory of the people of Israel when faced with danger or uncertainty during their four-decade long wanderings through the desert. By establishing the Law, He made certain that future generations would always be reminded: "When your son asks you in time to come, saying, 'What is the meaning of the testimonies, the statutes, and the judgments which the Lord our God has commanded you?' then you shall say to your son: 'We were slaves of Pharaoh in Egypt, and the Lord brought us out of Egypt with a mighty hand; and the Lord showed signs and wonders before our eyes, great and severe, against Egypt, Pharaoh, and all his household.'"(Deuteronomy 6:20-22)

And so, I begin the first book of my memoires. It is the first of three books that revisit the challenges I've faced from the very start of this journey: The beginning of the Universal Church of the Kingdom of God, the hard work of growing it over the last 35 years, the succession of battles and accomplishments that were marked by pivotal, unexpected events, and above all, personal spiritual experiences that I have never before revealed in such detail.

Nothing to Lose is not simply a recounting of the past. I don't know how to live in the past. I look ahead. And so, this work looks to the future with the goal of gathering and disclosing personal experiences as a foundation for the faith of Christians, and for those who feel lost.

This book does not follow precise chronological order. Most chapters are out of sequence, according to the subject matter. I cover topics individually, seeking to extract the practical teachings on belief in God's Word that I experienced in my daily life. This is not a typical narrative of people and events I encountered over the last several decades, because there are several close unnamed people who don't appear in the following pages. The main goal of this work is to record in my own words the moments of conviction that changed my life and that may help others to find a greater meaning for their own lives.

Nothing to Lose is mostly based on my memories and those of Ester, my loyal companion from the very beginning of this journey. With the help of journalist and writer Douglas Tavolaro, who has been with us for nine years, I have written my narrative with the aid of reports from those who first started following me, assistants and pastors, memories contributed by family and relatives, and old documents, news articles, and photos from those times. In some cases, I had to rely solely on my memory.

In the following pages, I have done my best to write about lessons I have learned from this walk of faith. I ask God to make my experiences useful for readers, helping them to make decisions about their own lives and to grab a hold of the most important thing in this world: the eternal salvation of their soul.

I thank God's Spirit for the opportunity to share my story with each one of you.

CHAPTER 1

ELEVEN DAYS IN JAIL

NO MATTER WHO GETS HURT

I enjoy admiring the sky—the sun, the clouds, the moon, the stars. They all form a perfect composition, a symbol of what is most sublime in the gift of perfection. The sky is a good representation of the transformation of a previously formless, empty planet.

Wherever I travel, I spend hours watching the blue horizon and meditating about God. Alone, I sit in a chair in silence without reading or hearing any sound, without talking to anyone. I usually do this at dawn. The sun warms my body. I meditate about divine promises, compassion, and will.

I look inside myself.

It is my moment with God. Jesus would "retire" to the desert to pray. No one would join him. He would set off alone to experience his spiritual intimacy. It was the nourishment of his soul. I follow that example. These moments of silence, when I admire the beauty of the sky, make me listen to God. They make me think. And they bring back memories.

The sky is also the expression of freedom. When I was young, imprisonment really scared me. I used to tell my siblings that I would rather take a beating from my father than not be allowed to leave the house. Being enclosed caused agony in me. What human being can lead a happy life without being able to exercise the freedom to come and go? Without the simple choice of entering or leaving any place whenever he or she wishes? It seems simple and elementary, but for one moment, try to imagine living your life with no control over your actions. It was the freedom that I sacrificed to witness a radical change in my path and in the future of the Universal Church.

In 1992, when I was in São Paulo, I used to preach every Wednesday and Sunday at a small, homely Church located on Promotor Gabriel Nettuzzi Peres Street in the district of Santo Amaro. At the time, that was the location of our largest Church in Brazil. I would usually go to the gathering with my wife, Ester, and my middle daughter Viviane, who was 17 years old at the time. She was the only one who lived with me. Cristiane, the oldest, was living and studying in the United States, as was Moisés, my adopted son.

It was a bright morning in São Paulo, a special Sunday as usual. I woke up early to read the Bible and prepare for the gathering.

The service lasted for two hours. I talked a lot about how important it is to maintain an alliance with God and how we should trust Him above all, in any situation, because everything that God does is good and is for our own good. At the end of the gathering, I prayed for everyone, pleaded that they all go home in peace and safety, and wished them a happy week. The service was wonderful. The word of salvation had been sowed. The spirit of faith had been transmitted in a lively way.

However, it was my turn to be tested in practice. It was my turn to prove the real size of my trust.

I left the altar, said goodbye to some pastors and, as was usual on the weekends, invited my friend Laprovita Vieira and his wife, Vera, for lunch at our house. I asked Laprovita to follow me in his car. It was early afternoon on May 24, 1992—more precisely, 1:30 p.m. How could that date and time be forgotten?

It was a period in which the Universal Church, my family, and I were under attack. Since our work started to grow, we had been targeted. The Roman Clergy had full power in Brazil, more so than at present. There were high-ranking politicians, economic and social elite businessmen, intellectuals, Supreme Court judges, and other authorities from the Judiciary Power who made decisions under the influence of the Catholic high command. The Curia would not accept the rise of a people who were free of the religious slavery imposed by it. But I never really observed that. My mission was a single one: to preach the truth of the Gospel to all who were suffering.

Even before purchasing the Record TV Network in November 1989, we had been victims of several types of abuse. The police had invaded my flat, the Church offices, and related companies that supported the evangelical work. I knew the persecution would never have an end, but never imagined that those aggressions would have me end up in prison.

My name was trashed for many years. For those who hated me, Bishop Macedo was synonymous with thief. That is still true to this day. A lot of people who do not even know me wish me harm. Granted, the Word of God had warned me about it. Many who converted changed their opinion once they learned about the work of the Church and my intentions. That was no problem—it was the same with Jesus. However, I never accepted the idea that the Brazilian justice system would be influenced by the will of the Vatican or by pressure from the press that was manipulated by them.

The Universal Church had already spread to four continents and was advancing unhindered. Souls were being won all over the world. Thousands of pastors and workers were raised, and the number of followers was multiplying. Record TV had been purchased only three years before. We were still putting the company in order, but it already showed great potential for development. Everyone knew that Record TV would follow the path of sustainable, irreversible growth, and this is what actually happened.

And I paid for all of that.

I drove a few blocks from the Church parking lot and, on São Benedito street, we heard a strange noise. The image seems fixed in my mind: dozens of police cars driving towards us. Ester asked me whether I had broken some traffic law.

"No, Ester. I am driving normally."

"So what's going on?" Ester asked.

There was no time to reply. The police in their cars, accelerating wildly, with their sirens sounding, told me to stop.

They waved violently. Some officers stuck their heads out of their car windows and shouted at me.

The car was surrounded. Machine guns, pistols, and a many heavy weapons were pointed at me and my family. What harm could we do? It was just Ester, my 17-year-old daughter, and me. I almost lost count of the number of officers. There were five sheriffs and 13 civil and federal agents.

I stopped the car and put my hands up. I could not understand what was going on. "My God, what is all this about?" I thought to myself. "My God!"

It all seemed more like a kidnapping than a police operation. I was immediately arrested and dragged towards one of the police cars. My Bible remained on the back seat, right next to Viviane. I did not resist, nor could I.

Laprovita, who was a federal congressman at the time, tried to ask the police to calm down. He showed his parliamentary card, which was thrown to the ground by the policemen. There was no calming down, only confusion and shouting all over the place. I felt like fighting with everyone to free myself and protect my family.

Before entering the police car, I swiftly looked back. For a few seconds I saw Ester and Viviane screaming, asking the police officers for an explanation, but nobody seemed to listen to them. A small commotion was happening in the road. The police car sped away with me arrested between two armed agents.

My family's expressions of despair are registered in my memory.

LORD, WHERE AM I?

That Sunday afternoon of 1992 I was on my way to prison. I did not know where I would be taken, only that I was on my way to be locked up. My legs were shaking. My heart was pounding, but I remained silent in the police car as it sped along. Despite the feeling of having lost all control, there was peace inside me. In a moment of carelessness, the policeman to my left let the handcuffs, that were supposed to be attached to my wrists, fall at my feet. They all appeared nervous, tense, and disorderly.

I could not see properly. I felt indignant. I wondered where my family was at that moment. I thought about Ester and Viviane, left in the middle of the road. I thought about the church. I thought about our people. I asked God to protect me. I asked Him to protect my family.

How do people face situations like this without God's protection? A thousand may fall at my side, and ten thousand at my right hand; but it shall not come near me. All alone in a hopeless battle against horses and chariots and a great army commanded by the King of Syria, the prophet Elisha saw an even greater army of horses and chariots of fire covering the mountains behind them. But he had to use his spiritual eyes to see this "invisible" army.

King Solomon's proverbs reveal God as a shield for the upright. A shield, defender, an aid, a shelter.

Sincerity has always been one of the pillars of the work of the Universal Church. From our very first days in the late 1970's, I have always reminded our pastors that a basis of our belief should be honesty before the people, and most importantly before God. I have always been that way.

I hate deceit, dishonesty, and hypocrisy. I would quit my ministry as a pastor or bishop if I had to resort to hypocrisy and emotional hype to get people to join the church. Pastors who cry on the altar only to manipulate the emotions of those watching, actors who will play any role—meek one moment and harsh the next—who use tricks to keep the doors of their church open, enrage me.

I refuse to change. Sincerity has always been the rule of my ministry and personal life.

Anyone close to me knows this to be so. I value truth above all, no matter the cost, even if it involves loss for the church—loss of members, offering, or anything else. It doesn't matter. Truth frees and sincere faith ensures that we will eventually rise to the top. This is how it has always been for me throughout the decades of doing the work of God.

I walk the path of the upright, as Solomon stated. Because of this, I trusted in God's protection in the midst of all the injustice and harassment during my arrest.

After arresting me on the street, the police car's first stop was the DEIC (State Department for Criminal Investigations). It was a 20-kilometer drive that took only a few minutes. I was wearing a grey suit, white shirt, and red tie, the same clothes I had worn for the meeting in Santo Amaro. The police pulled me out of the car and pushed me into the building. In the few steps between the car and the entrance I noticed a cameraman wearing a vest from one of the main TV stations in the country. He was the only one from the press there. Strange, isn't it?

I was informed of the warrant for my arrest only after I was inside this building. My mind drifted: Arrest warrant? How? What possible legal basis could they have for this? How could a judge authorize this? How could they justify my arrest? What were they up to?

Many questions went unanswered.

I was placed inside a DEIC investigation room, waited for hours, and noticed continuous movement.

I—a person who's always careful to pay my bills on time, who panics at the thought of making late payments—was in jail. I was handcuffed like a dangerous criminal. Then some policemen told me I would be sent to another location where I would be locked up for weeks.

I arrived at the Vila Leopoldina police station, west of São Paulo, in the early evening. That was my address throughout my eleven days of imprisonment.

That is where I experienced the most terrible eleven days of my life. Eleven days of loneliness. One after the other. My Lord, the greatest of all Spirits, would guide me through this desert. I begged for light in those moments when the darkness of hell was overwhelming.

At the station I was taken out of the car and quickly escorted by investigators from the civil police, two men who made a point of showing the guns on their waists.

We walked up to the last door in the main corridor of the station. An iron gate separated the hallway from a corridor of cells—the border between a life of freedom and the agony of imprisonment, between good citizens and those who allowed themselves to sink into a life of crime. Shattered honor. Robbed of dignity.

The iron gate swung open for me.

"Lord, where am I?" I thought to myself over and over again.

Joseph had been put in prison. Jeremiah was thrown into a dungeon. Daniel was shut up in a den. Peter knew the sorrow of a prisoner while the church persevered in prayer and a light shone in the prison. Paul and Silas were thrown into a dungeon and beaten, and the prison shook when they prayed.

How do we react with faith in our real-life dramas?

The four cells were crowded. More than 20 prisoners filled the cramped space. I saw the cell where I would spend my first night behind bars, and walked in.

My eyes took in the stifling surroundings. It was dark. No windows, light, or sun. No sky.

The air was heavy. It had an overpowering, unpleasant smell. Now I could understand why Brazilian inmates felt such disgust for prison.

I stood almost motionless, as if time had stopped. Some prisoners recognized me. "Bishop! Bishop!" one of the guards called out. He told me I needed to talk to the sheriff in charge of the district, Darci Sassi. He was polite and explained the rules of the jail and what was expected of prisoners. I bowed my head and agreed to everything, without questioning a thing. The sheriff tried to comfort me by saying that this was the way justice worked; it did not always work as it should. I looked deeply into his eyes and said that I would face it all with my head held high because I had faith in God.

I was led back into the cell. There was no place to sleep—the beds were already taken and the floor was covered with mattresses. This cell was for white-collar prisoners with degrees. The prisoner-in-charge approached me and also explained the rules.

There was one bathroom for all of us. He advised me to wash my hands in the old sink before flushing the toilet.

I sat down in a small empty space in the cell waiting for what the night would bring. Hours later I was given a small mattress, and with the help of some prisoners, arranged a corner for myself. I stretched the small mattress on the floor between two bunk beds that had already been taken.

That was the beginning of my first night behind bars.

I had no dinner. I simply nourished my thoughts. As I lay there struggling to sleep, memories flashed through my mind.

I went back to thinking about the greatness of God and His plans. How do we process events that strike us like lightning in the middle of a storm? I thought about the Holy Spirit's power to free people. I recalled the thousands of miracles I had witnessed in the Universal Church since I had started preaching at the pavilion in Méier, Rio de Janeiro. I recalled the former funeral parlor that had been turned into a warm church, a platform for repentance and new lives.

Maracanã stadium and other stadiums around Brazil had been packed with crowds of people receiving the greatest of all miracles: salvation of their souls.

Man's weakness and God's faithfulness. The psalmist said that God gives justice to the oppressed. I was oppressed. Ester, my daughters, and my family were oppressed. The Lord sets prisoners free, raises those who have fallen, and loves justice. I was pleading for justice.

But I had to wait. I had to trust with all my strength.

A vow is a vow!

It was stuffy that night. When I tried to close my eyes, I would find a prisoner stepping over me, even stepping on my small mattress. I was in the pathway to the toilet. At dawn I was told that I would see several visitors that day. Ester was the first to see me that morning.

I was calm. After a quick black coffee, I was taken to a small room in the station where I would be more at ease during my visits. Ester entered slowly through the door and broke down. She looked exhausted and could not stand seeing me in jail. She cried in silence.

Tears of injustice.

"You're coming home today, aren't you?" she asked.

"I don't know. I don't think so," I replied, in anger.

When she had calmed down she told me of that night's pain and how it had united her and Viviane. The thought of it disturbed me.

The shock of prison was so bad for Ester, that until today it's as if it happened yesterday. It was a scare that broadsided us both.

That meeting with Ester gave me the strength to endure prison. When nobody could calm me down, she always had a word of support. A look, a hug, a touch. I usually say that Ester was in prison with me for those 11 days. She was the second leg that gave me support—my balance. Without her, it would have been much harder to overcome the many obstacles.

Before asking for clean clothes and toiletries, I asked Ester for a Bible. Without the embraces of such a loving wife I would not have had the strength to make it through those days in prison, deprived as I was of the Word of God.

The resolve I needed was in what God's Spirit would tell me as I read the His holy Word. I needed help, comfort, and guidance, a light upon my path and a lamp to my feet. Ever since I surrendered my life to God the Bible has been my compass in life, guided my attitudes, values, and beliefs.

The Bible helped me understand that there was a clear promise in the midst of the chaos that surrounded me. Right away a passage stood out as evidence: "In my distress I called upon the Lord, and cried out to my God; He heard my voice from His temple, and my cry came before Him, even to His ears." (Psalm 18:6).

The value of a promise became even clearer to me. The value of the Word. Even the prisoners who shared my cell honored the word. The world of crime is one in which criminals create and follow rules based on their word. There are no signed papers or notaries. Everything works on the basis of the word, and no one dares to break those laws because they know the price is death.

That's life among criminals. I thought of man's relationship with God. There is no way that a vow made by God could fail. That was all I needed to define my faith and know what I wanted and what I believed, without hesitation.

But time belongs to God.

Monday morning I was still receiving visits from church colleagues. Bishops and pastors embraced me and tried to raise my spirits, and slowly I learned the truth about the absurd events that had occurred.

First of all, I learned that the arrest was supposed to have taken place inside the church where the meeting had been held that Sunday morning. I could only imagine what it would have been like if the police had intruded on our service. What would people's reaction have been? The pastors and assistants could have reacted and caused tragic consequences. And so I came to the conclusion that God had protected His Church.

Only after consulting with my lawyers did I understand the reasons for my arrest. I was being accused of charlatanism, being a faith-healer, and fraud.

Charlatanism is the practice of exploiting the public, takes advantage of the weak-minded, and falsely pretending to have skills or powers. According to Brazilian law, being a faith-healer means you are practicing medicine illegally or pretending to treat disease by means of spiritism or the occult. Fraud is when a person lies or intentionally deceives others to take advantage of them for personal gain.

That is why the court ordered my imprisonment. They thought I would skip bail and leave the country, even after we proved that I had a permanent residence and was diligently cooperating in all interrogations. But the most revolting thing, was to be accused of crimes I had not committed.

When I heard the charges my anger rose. The prophets were healers. Elijah raised a child from the dead after multiplying her oil and flour. Elisha healed a war hero, a general, from leprosy. Hannah, who had become bitter for years, was healed of infertility, giving birth to Samuel. Hezekiah made a bold prayer to God and cried bitterly, and was saved from a terminal illness.

The Lord Jesus was a healer. He had ordered a paralytic to stand up, pick up his mat, and go home. A woman who suffered from a chronic hemorrhage was healed at the touch of His garments. A tormented Canaanite child was healed by her mother's persistence. A blind man's eyes were opened when mud was placed on them. It couldn't be any clearer. The disciples healed. They would lay their hands on the sick and make them well. Healing was common in the early Church.

What I do today is no more than preach this same faith: absolute belief in the supernatural power of prayer. There are millions of people in Brazil and all over the world who can prove that this faith produces miracles. Yes, they do exist, and they are real in the lives of the people of the Universal Church.

Because of this and their personal experiences with God, many people have remained true to these beliefs. They have seen uncommon things when no one else would give them the time of day—not the government, not the authorities, not even their own families. They were outcasts who found something to live for and at present are successful and happy men and women. Who's going to tell them that they were healed and saved by a fake faith-healer and charlatan? Why accuse a person who has only offered help to the disadvantaged?

On the other hand, how many millions, or billions, of dollars has the Universal Church saved the government of Brazil, through its work of deliverance and healing? Countless children and adults would otherwise be crowding into public hospitals, waiting to be treated. Many have spiritual illnesses that cannot be cured through the efforts of physicians and nurses.

The church's work in prisons from the north to south of this country has greatly benefitted the nation. I can recall two instances of this. In one case, two women with expensive jewelry and clothes were walking past the shop windows of some well-known stores on an upscale street in São Paulo. They were engaged in conversation when a young man passed by on his way to work, and overheard them criticizing me. They were accusing me of being a thief who loved exploiting the poor. The young man could not hold himself back.

"Excuse me ladies, but you have no idea what you're talking about. You know, if it weren't for Bishop Macedo, I'd be robbing you right now. I'm an ex-felon and the Universal Church of the Kingdom of God helped me to change," he stated. The women were dumbfounded. He excused himself and went off to work.

Another example in Rio de Janeiro happened when a business executive hailed a taxi at the airport and gave his home address to the driver. As soon as traffic slowed down, the driver started talking. Without asking the passenger about his religious beliefs, he started criticizing religion and attacking the Universal Church. His lengthy tirade ended with a, "Isn't that right?" In reply, he was asked to pull over.

"You should thank God for that Church… I used to rob taxis. If not for them you could have been robbed and maybe even killed by now. Goodbye," he said angrily. The man paid for the ride up to that point and took another taxi home.

The conclusion is simple. How many Brazilians would be in prison at this very moment—with the public footing the bill—or carrying out kidnappings, robberies, murders, and other atrocities were it not for the intense rehabilitative work of the Universal Church?

But the question that would not go away in the hours after my first visit to the police station was: Why am I being detained for something I didn't do?

David, Goliath, and me

The days lingered on. In spite of the revolt that ate away at me, I tried to concentrate, and remain peaceful and thoughtful the entire time.

This was the only way to overcome the indignity of prison. When there was no one from the outside to talk to, I would spend hours talking with God and meditating on scripture. I never let go of the Word of God even for a moment.

The room reserved for visits soon became my permanent space. The police chief said he didn't want any trouble among the other prisoners because of the number of visitors I was having. But even so, I would walk in the yard with the other prisoners during exercise time.

I began to win their friendship. I was surprised by their sympathy and hospitality. There were 22 prisoners, all lawyers, physicians, judges, businessmen, and politicians. We all got along peacefully. I talked about the Lord Jesus and salvation to many of them, even to some guards.

As a result, to this day I encourage the work of the church's prison groups. I make a point of closely following up on the results of thousands of our pastors who are pointing the way out for inmates, wasting away in the prison system, on a daily basis. This is where salvation takes place—when society has excluded them, in a moment of extreme pain when wives, children, and friends have turned their backs on them. There is no one left but Jesus. As a result, a new life comes into being.

The love, support and spiritual help of the church for prisoners and their families, has transformed many. Men and women have found comfort in the pit of despair, even for those in solitary confinement for disruptive behavior or death threats. The Spirit of God, through the gospel, is rescuing these people with shocking transformations of character, turnarounds in personality, and radical changes in habits, behavior, and lifestyle. They become new men and women, free from the oppression of a life of crime, and actually assimilate back into society through the power of faith in Jesus.

During the first week at the police station, I authorized the press to photograph me behind bars. I was sitting at the back of the cell, legs crossed, reading the Bible. I was wearing a white, short-sleeved shirt and gray trousers that Ester had brought me. I patiently allowed some reporters access to me. In the first interview after my arrest, I spoke about what I had been reflecting upon over the previous days—thoughts from scripture.

In front of a television crew, I said that I understood this to be a baptism of fire. Though I did not deserve it, I viewed myself as one of the Apostles, since I was experiencing the same things they went through in ancient times. It was a privilege to suffer as other men of God had suffered, for a Lord that I embraced with all my understanding.

I said more. I stated that at the moment we may not understand, but I believed that it would all turn out for the good—the good of the Universal Church, the good of God's work, and the good of the faith in each one of us.

And yet, I so wanted to go back home.

Time crawled on. Five days in jail and still nothing. The lawyers did not come with a single piece of positive news. Every request for my release had been denied. Freedom seemed so far away.

Alone at night, I would think of the persecution I was going through and how it was dragging on. I would cry out to God for peace of body and soul. I whispered prayers. I prayed in thought. I prayed non-stop.

Letting off steam with God has always been one of my weapons—both offensive and defensive.

I defended myself by getting on my knees to face every moment of despair. At times like these the heavens open up for those who cry out to God for help. God is not far away. Though He is eternal and dwells "in the high and holy place" God is with "him who has a contrite and humble spirit". (Isaiah 57:15).

I attacked by stretching out my hands to the doubts that oppressed my thoughts. It was a tireless war between light and darkness, faith and the uncertainty of fear. The Jews were led out of Egyptian slavery by Moses, and then died in the desert for doubting. What would normally be a two-month journey to the land promised by God, lasted more than 40 years because of their endless murmuring.

My faith would win over doubt. My prayers pointed me in one direction: I had to transform my problems into great opportunities. God did not make David king—Goliath the giant, who insulted the people of Israel, did that. Abraham made use of Sarah's infertility to prove that he had faith in God. Challenges, battles, and difficulties are simply opportunities for growth.

And so it happened with me in jail.

The extended period of time it took for the Justice Department to authorize my release brought about the most surprising circumstances. A growing number of people—celebrities, common people, and even critics—began to support me. A constant flow of statements in favor of my freedom began to come in from authorities, politicians, artists, and even leaders of other churches.

A unity of the Universal Church was ignited.

Pastors, blue collar workers, and people in general started holding vigils at the door of the Vila Leopoldina police station. I began to sense the faith surrounding that place. I was aware of the prayers of thousands of followers in my favor.

After seven days in jail, the chief officer on duty, Silvia Cavalcanti, expressed her concern about the growing number of protesters and asked me to record a radio message to calm them down. I immediately complied with her request.

There were rumors that members of the Universal Church were planning to break into the jail. Obviously, the police feared anything like that.

I asked the people to continue their "chains of prayer" and fasting, asking God to get me out as soon as possible, but also to help our people to stay calm and to use their heads. I thanked each one of them for their concern in the midst of so much trouble. Interestingly, I was calming the nerves of all them, when I needed calming down, myself.

One day, more than 1000 protestors were at the door of the police station, and surround the jail in a huge chain, holding hands. I was in bed when I received the news.

I was touched by their spirit.

My body was showing signs of exhaustion. I ate almost nothing and drank only water, lots of water. My effort to keep emotions in check robbed me of my appetite.

I could often hear songs of the church being sung by protesters from the church outside the police station. The officer in charge told me that he couldn't count the number of frail, elderly ladies he could see crying and praying for hours on end. Day and night, sometimes until very late, circles of people formed on the pavement, holding hands, crying out to God for me.

I will never meet most of these people or know their names, but I will be forever grateful to each one of them for the rest of my life.

At the end of the first week in jail, I left the station for a court hearing. I was placed in the back seat of a squad car with my Bible in my hand. In court I was face to face with the judge that had signed my arrest warrant. He was a young man in his early 30s, the assistant to the criminal court judge that had issued the warrant. Halfway through the interrogation the judge asked an intriguing and offensive question that had no connection with the accusations brought against me.

He wanted to know whether there had been a decrease in the attendance of the church. I was straightforward. I said no, on the contrary, numbers had been multiplying. In fact, the churches had become overcrowded with people curious about the news and in support of the church's struggle.

Another fact also caught my attention in court. Strangely, a man in robes, most probably a priest or member of some Vatican ecclesiastical order, listened to my interrogation and took extensive notes. No one should have been allowed to attend this hearing, but that day, things were different.

To this very day that scene has not been fully explained to me.

A VOICE WITHIN

I was revolted. Not with the authorities, institutions, government, or police, but with injustice. Jesus was revolted. On His own, He had driven the money-changers from the Temple in Jerusalem with a whip. It was impossible to put up with so much inequality. Back at the police station the agony stretched on. One day I received an unexpected visitor from Rio de Janeiro, my mother, Eugênia Macedo Bezerra, who at the time was 71. As soon as she saw me in jail she wept inconsolably. I placed my hand on her shoulder and said:

"Calm down, Mother. God is with us."

"I believe that, my son," she replied and hugged me. "I pray for you every evening, dear."

Whenever she entered or left the station, an army of reporters surrounded her, asking for interviews. It was a shock that was difficult for someone of her age to bear. My sister Eris Bezerra—who lived with my mother for the last days of her life—recalls that the press continually humiliated the Universal Church and our family with their hostile articles, which hurt my mother deeply.

But she stood firm by my side, always encouraging me to push forward.

The unconditional love from my dearly missed mother, who passed away five years later, further strengthened me while I was behind bars. The promise of Isaiah the prophet is clear: Though a mother may forget about her nursing child, the son of her womb, yet God will not forget me.

My name, like the names of all who have faith, is engraved in God's palm.

On the eleventh day in prison, I woke up confident that my nightmare was at an end. The judge had finally accepted my habeas corpus. The São Paulo criminal court had unanimously voted for my release.

Relief. I took a deep breath. God, at last, had answered my cry.

I did not know whether to laugh or cry. All I wanted to do was pack my things and leave. I wanted my freedom. And it came through the main door of the police station.

Before leaving, I asked the pastors and assistants to hand out dozens of Bibles to the prisoners I was leaving behind. In the cell, with Ester's help, I collected my clothes and personal possessions. I put on a dark blue suit and white shirt. One by one I said goodbye to the guards and my cellmates, and thanked them for our 11 days together. And then I left.

The police and investigators from that district organized a human barrier to hold back the crowds right after 7pm. It was pandemonium. I was almost crushed by the crowd. Everyone wanted to record interviews and photograph me. I could hear shouts of celebration from the members of the church. They were euphoric, celebrating and excitedly trying to greet me.

It's impossible to forget that scene.

We quickly left the police station. It was time to go home. Actually, it was time to go to the church. I could not step a foot into my home before thanking God for having freed me from so much suffering. I decided to go straight to the Santo Amaro church.

"I left the church and went to prison, so now I'll go from prison back to the church," I told my brother Celso Bezerra, who gave directions to the driver from the passenger seat.

In the back seat I held on firmly to Ester's arm. My wife's warmth, God's freedom. It was impossible not to recall a unique fact: exactly four months earlier I had started writing a song inspired by the words of the prophet Isaiah, in which he encouraged the people of Israel to trust God as they went out to do battle with their enemies.

On January 10th of the year of my arrest, the song was finished and was given the title "I Am with You." The lyrics were the exact comfort that my spirit needed.

You whom I took from the abyss
From the farthest place of the earth
I declared, you are My servant

I've chosen you
Do not fear for I'll not, reject you

I am with you
Don't fear, nor be afraid
I am your God, I am your real friend
I'll strengthen you, and I will protect you
And I'll uphold you with My righteous hand

They will be completely ashamed and destroyed
Those who persecute you
They will be all reduced to nothing
Those who make war against you

I am with you
Don't fear, nor be afraid
I am your God, I am your real friend
I'll strengthen you, and I will protect you
And I'll uphold you with My righteous hand
I am with you[1]

The song was my life, what I most needed to hear from God at that moment.

---

1 *A quem livrei do abismo/ Do lugar mais longínquo da Terra/ Eu disse tu és meu servo/ Eu te escolhi/ Não temas porque não te rejeitei/ Eu sou contigo/ Não temas nem te espantes/ Eu sou teu Deus/ Eu sou o teu amigo/ Te fortaleço e te ajudo/ E te sustento com o Meu poder/ Eis que serão/ Envergonhados e confundidos/ Todos que te perseguirem/ Serão todos reduzidos a nada/ Aqueles que demandam contra ti // Eu sou contigo/ Não temas nem te espantes/ Eu sou teu Deus/ Eu sou teu amigo/ Te fortaleço e te ajudo/ E te sustento com o Meu poder/ Estou contigo.*

I was almost unaware of time as we drove from the police station to the church. When I got out of the car I slowly walked up to the altar.

The altar is the highest place in a church—a place of sacrifice, surrender, and deliverance, a place of closeness with the Lord.

I was back in my hiding place, the hiding place of all men of God—my protection, my shield, my refuge.

It was all over. God was with me.

I knelt with my back to the people, closed my eyes and said to God:

"Thank you. Thank you so much, O Lord."

When I stood up, I saw the people, a standing crowd that disappeared into the back of the church—pastors, assistants, and people. Men, women, and children. They all applauded nonstop. I was silent for a few seconds. All I said was:

"All honor to my God."

A few days later, at home, I did what I continue to do up to this very day in moments of meditation. I thought about the meaning of what I had experienced over those 11 days. Imagine going through all those painful moments 20 years later, after the Department of Justice had declared me completely innocent. One by one, every criminal charge was proven false. I was acquitted of every charge. And yet, every now and then, they still attempt to repeat the same accusations.

It is not easy to put up with. When I suffered the first attacks, right after purchasing Record TV, it became such a burden that I wished I had never even bought it. It was very tough. I thought about it a number of times when I was behind bars.

"Why Lord? Why? What is it that You want from me?" I asked deep within. "Could it be that God was no longer with me? Had He abandoned me? What had become of His mercy and power? What about all I had preached over the years?"

I wanted to believe in my mind, but often something seemed to resist in my heart.

I have always looked for help in the Word of God, and assurance and trust would soon expel the doubts from within. It was an act of the Holy Spirit Himself. "This will go away. You'll win!" a loud voice would shout within me, in my mind.

In the face of bitterness, conflict would rise to the surface. My feelings would struggle with my faith. But the Bible would bring renewal: Joshua was told to be strong and courageous and to take possession of God's promise. Strong and courageous. That's what I would be.

I followed this path of faith. And my life and the 35 years of the Universal Church are proof of the faith that transforms situations and raises us up to heaven.

CHAPTER 2

How I found God

THE FATE OF MY SOUL

"Bishop, a miracle just happened, Jesus saved me! Since hearing the teachings of the Lord, I've decided to face the truth. I'd been knocked down, but now I'm up. Our Lord had compassion on me and saved me. I'm so thankful I'm saved."

(Marina de Fátima Conceição, 39 years old – São Paulo, SP)

I read these words with joy. It was just one of thousands of comments that I get every week on my blog. Most comments are people's opinions, thoughts, or simply a reaffirmation of messages posted every day. But nothing moves me more than reading about experiences such as the one described above. I don't have words to express how overwhelming the sense of satisfaction is. Before I realize it, my eyes are full of tears, at peace knowing that another soul has been rescued from hell.

A priceless achievement expressed in simple and true terms. This is my biggest reward. It makes all the daily sacrifices, the endless and difficult battles against the Kingdom of Darkness, worth it. It's an invisible, never-ending, bloody battle between God and the devil for each soul.

I always say that a life saved is priceless. "What would a man give in exchange for his soul?" Jesus asked his disciples. When two brothers fought over an inheritance, Jesus reinforced the value of eternal life. He ended the parable with a harsh warning: "Fool! This night your soul will be required of you; then whose will those things be which you have provided?" (Luke 12:20)

Death on this planet is the end of the line. The Bible makes it strikingly clear that nothing and no one can change the course of a soul after its last breath on earth. Two angels carried the soul of the beggar Lazarus to spiritual rest in God's kingdom. But the rich man was in agony, tormented in hell. Hell. Yes, that's the exact term used in scriptures. A great chasm separated the two. Eternal life and eternal death.

Salvation is of great value. But the joy that comes over me when winning a new soul for God is also met with a profound sadness. I think of the multitudes of people that have not yet been reached by the message of redemption in the Lord Jesus. "My Father, what should I do to reach as many people as possible?" I ask God insistently, night and day.

Among the comments of readers who have been saved, I also receive pleas for help. The words below, also written on my blog, reveal a small portrait of the agony of those who live in darkness and suffering. It's a desperate cry from someone who doesn't know what to do, who doesn't see a way out from their problems.

A cry for help.

"Bishop, I need your help urgently. My situation is a mess. I feel empty and I want to die. I see shadows and hear voices that don't exist. I suffer from insomnia and am very scared. My husband left me with our two children. I can't bear to leave my room and I think of suicide all day long. Everything is going wrong and I have no more hope. The only thing left is death. For the love of God, help me!"

(A desperate friend, 41 years old – Londrina, PR)

I understand the pain of each one of these people. Every single one without exception. Man or woman, rich or poor, college educated or illiterate, of any race or ethnicity, religious or not. It doesn't matter. They all carry groans of anguish that echo in my mind. Wherever I am and wherever I go, in Brazil or in other countries, I can see on their faces the torment, depression, frustration, trauma, and more that eats away at them every day.

Just speaking of the immensity of this challenge, the challenge that gives my life meaning, causes my heart to race. My purpose in this world is to save souls.

Whoever is saved wants to save. This is what drives my faith and is the true spirit of the Universal Church of the Kingdom of God since it was founded. And since then, the altars and the walls of our churches have been inscribed with the words, "Jesus Christ is the Lord."

I am driven by this desire for one reason, because of one moment exactly 48 years ago, that radically transformed my life: my encounter with God.

Beginning on the road of faith was not easy. During my childhood and especially through adolescence, I was searching for answers. My thoughts of God were those of extreme respect and reverence, but He was someone distant, unreachable, and impossible to touch.

I was born into a Catholic family. My father, Henrique Francisco Bezerra, from Penedo, a city in the semi-arid state of Alagoas, was a very diligent farm worker. He always said that he believed in both God and his "saints." He was a member of the Masons, a secret religious brotherhood that spread throughout Brazil in the middle of the last century.

My father was 32 years old when he met my mother, Eugênia, who was a humble and demure 16 year old from Rio das Flores, a small country town in the state of Rio de Janeiro, on the border of Minas Gerais. She was also from a traditional Catholic family. She soon became pregnant for the first time. There were many pregnancies to come, all of them difficult. Within their 54 years of marriage, my mother became pregnant 33 times. She had 16 miscarriages and lost 10 who were born premature. Seven survived.

I was born at home, with the help of my maternal grandmother, Clementina Macedo, as the midwife. At that time, it was common to use midwives, especially in the countryside, where there were no doctors or nurses. It was on the Sunday of Carnival, when the explosion of a boiler in one of the milk-cooperatives close by shook the city. The scare made my mother, who lived next to the site of the accident, go into labor.

I was born on February 18, 1945.

I was the fourth child, the second oldest son. All of us were raised strictly, under the harsh rule of our father. Discipline was a sacred rule at home. My mother was the protector of the home, the woman who raised us with love and such great zeal, that even as teenagers, we wouldn't rebel. She taught me the Lord's Prayer, and in her own way, she taught me to believe in God. I was born into, raised and trained in this dead and uncommitted faith. It wasn't the fault of my parents, but simply their lack of knowledge of spiritual things.

This seed of belief accompanied me in the years to come. Every time I was in danger—when I got into some kind of mischief that would certainly bring upon a serious beating by my father—I would repeat a phrase of protection. I'd run to my room or the bathroom, shut my eyes tight, put my hands together, and whisper two or three times:

"God is great. Lord Jesus Christ help me! God is great. Lord Jesus Christ help me!"

This phrase was my "lucky charm" in the period before my conversion. I thought it protected me from embarrassing situations, like when the other kids my age made fun of me at school because of my disability. I was born with a genetic defect on my hand. My index fingers are crooked and my thumbs are thin. None move freely, only the other three fingers of each hand have a normal range of motion. My paternal grandmother was born with missing fingers and I inherited this birth defect.

I confess that I often had an inferiority complex. I considered myself the ugly duckling in my school and family, and I was always made fun of. People liked to call me "pinky finger" which embarrassed me to no end. I felt like I couldn't do anything right. But even though I felt embarrassed, that didn't stop me from leading a peaceful life. As a child, nothing that bothered me could make me question God or took away the peace I had inside.

And yet, I had no commitment to faith when I was a young. I enjoyed making fun of the beliefs of evangelicals. When the pastors and members of the Assemblies of God church gathered to pray and evangelize at São Cristóvão, a traditional leisure area in the Rio de Janeiro neighborhood where I lived with my parents, I would ride by on my bicycle to make fun of them.

"Hallelujah, Hallelujah! I eat 'n drink, so what's it to ya!" I would shout, laughing while I pedaled faster so I wouldn't get into trouble.

But when I was alone with my thoughts, I was lost in unanswered questions. I thought that both good and evil came from the same place: God. If something was good, it must be a divine blessing, but if something was evil, it had to be a punishment from God. All the while I was going through the adventures of youth—my first crushes, friendships, going to dances with all the flirting and emotional thrills that inevitably left me with an abysmal and inexplicable feeling of emptiness. Nothing that I heard about God satisfied me. Many things just did not make sense.

During the days I was held at the police station in May, 1992, the Bible was always with me. The voice of God guided me in times of pain and injustice.

Protesting against my imprisonment, members of the Universal Church held hands and encircled the Legislative Assembly in São Paulo.

The police station in São Paulo, where I spent 11 days waiting for a court decision.

Policemen treated me like a dangerous criminal when they took me to give statements at the court.

Meditating on the Bible gave me comfort and inner strength behind bars.

Upon my release, a few steps from the street with my brother Celso (right) and former deputy Laprovita Vieira.

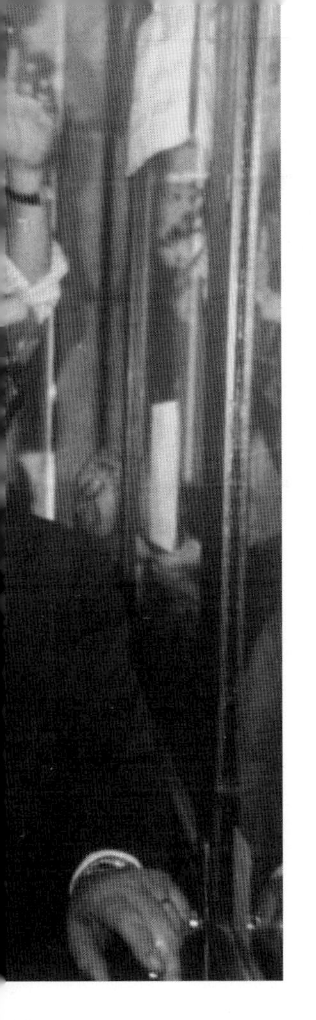

The church in Santo Amaro where I performed services before being arrested and right after my release.

In the first meeting after being released, I thanked God's Spirit for His protection. After the prayer, I hugged Ester, who stood by me during all those hard days.

Photos I took of dawn in Portugal and the horizon over the sea in the United States. "Heaven is my throne, and the earth is my footstool" (Isaiah 66.1).

I was born and spent the first years of my life in the small town of Rio das Flores. During my childhood and youth, I travelled back and forth between the interior of Rio de Janeiro and Minas Gerais.

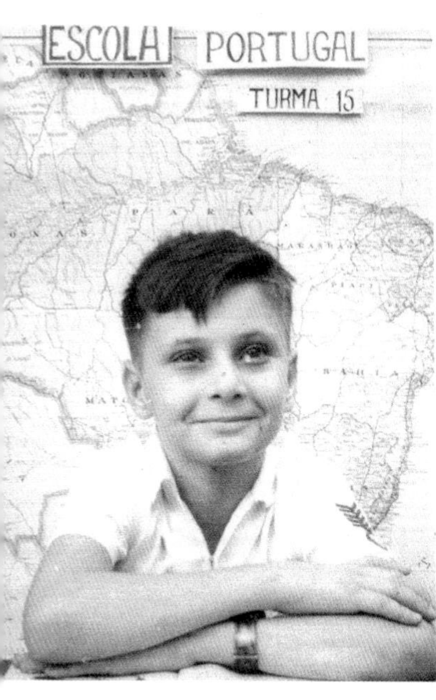
ESCOLA PORTUGAL
TURMA 15

Since she was young, Ester was always friendly and elegant. For me, her greatest beauty is her relationship with God.

Above: At a family party with my father, uncles, siblings and cousins in Simão Pereira. Below: On a trip to Caxambu, both cities in the interior of Minas Gerais.

It was one of the happiest moments of my life, our wedding day. Ester and I with my father Henrique, and my mother Eugênia, better known as Dona Geninha.

Ester and I on our honeymoon. Those were moments of joy and pleasure that, despite so much hardship, lasted throughout the years.

At work in the State Lottery.

Presidência da República — Secretaria de Planejamento
FUNDAÇÃO INSTITUTO BRASILEIRO DE GEOGRAFIA E ESTATÍSTICA - IBGE
ESCOLA NACIONAL DE CIÊNCIAS ESTATÍSTICAS

CARTEIRA N.º 164
O PORTADOR ESTÁ MATRICULADO SOB O
N.º 273053 2a. SÉRIE DO
CURSO de Bacharelado
GUANABARA 20 03 75
ALUNO
DIRETOR

My student ID from the Statistical Sciences National School in Rio. The dream of preaching the Gospel tugged at me day and night.

Learning about Jesus?

When I was 15 years old, on Good Friday, I was "dragged" off to find Jesus. Not my Jesus. The Dead Jesus.

I say that I was dragged because Good Friday forces people to mourn the death of someone who is alive. I didn't have that type of discernment then. I was enveloped by this emotional faith and was taken to the local Catholic Church.

The parish on São Januário de Santo Agostinho Street, on the way to the Vasco da Gama stadium in São Cristóvão, was full. The place was decorated with candles and flowers for the holy day. When I walked in, I saw the image of Jesus's body stretched out on a table and dozens of people praying around it. They repeated words without thinking about what they were really saying.

It was a shocking image. Jesus Christ, bloody and nailed to the cross. I was in this ceremony worshiping the Dead Jesus, as he was called by the priests.

My question was unavoidable:

"Who needs more help here, me or him?"

I kept repeating that question to myself, completely outraged. I didn't understand how so many people could kneel, bow, pray, and weep for an image that was so powerless. An image that created more pain, pity, and compassion, than faith or conviction that your prayers could be answered. Wasn't I in front of a God who could do everything? Where was this Lord I had heard about? Where was the invincible God Almighty? Where was the Lord of greatness and glory? How could He help me? Wasn't He the creator of the heavens and the earth? How could this image I was seeing be true?

Much later, these thoughts led me to understand the evil of idolatry. Millions and millions of people are enslaved by believing in something that doesn't work. I know that many sincere people believe in these images—I was one of them, carrying the pictures of my saints in my wallet, but this is not what the Bible teaches. The Holy Spirit brought this to my mind on that Good Friday. I wondered whether I should pray for myself, or for that dying image that was suffering on the table in front of the crowd of weeping devotees. It didn't make any sense. It was like an insult to my intelligence.

Now I understand that we shouldn't pray to saints and images saints for a simple reason: they are unable to do anything for us. They were once ordinary people who served God as faithful Christians do today. The miracles that happen in life, such as those that are recorded in the Bible, happened only because of the power of the Holy

Spirit and no one else, because He dwells in all of those who believe today.

The apostles, for example, never claimed to be mediators between God and men. Peter rejected being treated as a supernatural being: "And as Peter was coming in, Cornelius met him, and fell down at his feet, and worshipped him. But Peter took him up, saying, Stand up; I myself also am a man." (Acts 10:25-26)

The Bible is clear: the only mediator between men and God is Jesus. "Nor is there salvation in any other, for there is no other name under heaven given among men by which we must be saved." (Acts 4:12) This opposition to the worship of saints is not a matter of disrespecting the faith of one religion or another, but is simply what needs to be said based on the truth. The truth that sets us free. Not my truth, but the truth of God's Word.

When I was still a teen, during my sporadic visits to churches, I'd watch priests from a distance. To me, they were holy men, pure and without blame, representatives of God on earth. They swung their incense burners, blessed the sacrament, and gave the sacramental bread. They wore white robes with chains and gold crucifixes hanging around their necks. Archbishop, monsignor, and cardinal were imposing names synonymous with purity, so I thought at that time.

Recent years have unfortunately, proved me wrong—I say that without generalizing or accusing all priests of the same behavior, but the crimes of pedophilia that have been uncovered in the Catholic church are beyond disgusting and abhorrent. Even worse, is the criminal manner in which Church representatives shield these cowardly acts. Granting impunity to anyone who sexually abuses children is one of the greatest travesties of mankind. There are thousands of cases around the world still unresolved.

In the Universal Church, we discipline pastors involved in any kind of immorality without mercy. We have already had cases of pastors involved in pedophilia that were immediately expelled from the church. There was no discussion, negotiation, or any chance of concealing such atrocity. The pastor's origin, position, or seniority in the church does not matter. With a proven charge, any pedophile pastor is immediately expelled as a servant of God and we do all in our power to help the judicial system condemn the criminal.

HOSTAGE OF THE UNCERTAINTY

My search for God continued throughout my teens. In 1961, at 17 years old, I already had a good job with Rio de Janeiro's lottery commission[2]. I started my career in civil service with the help of our state's former governor, Carlos Lacerda, and my mother's persistence for him to grant jobs for her two sons. I happily took on the responsibilities of being an office boy, one of which was serving coffee to the board of directors.

Life was going along smoothly until all of a sudden, an illness shook our family.

My elder sister, Elcy, developed chronic asthmatic bronchitis. She and her new husband had moved into the house next door, literally sharing a wall with us. Some days, especially the coldest days of winter, were torture for us all. Elcy would gasp for breath, desperate for air.

---

2 *Since gambling is illegal in Brazil, the lottery system is a government run organization.*

My mother and sisters wouldn't know what to do. They would fly into a panic, holding her hands, massaging her chest, fanning the air, shouting, but nothing worked. Elcy could not breathe. Too often, after much frantic struggling, she would eventually faint. She'd lay unconscious, and it seemed as if she wouldn't come back. The seizures would strike throughout the day, but the most terrifying were in the middle of the night. Those scenes are etched into my memory. Poor Elcy had lost so much weight because of so many medications, that she was just skin and bones.

Elcy's disease shook the whole family and everyone was trying to find a solution for her. Medical treatments were of no use. Our prayers to the saints didn't work either. Our family decided that it was time to turn to a spiritist center near our old house in São Cristóvão for help, called Santo Antônio de Pádua.

I kept believing in what I knew of God, and agreed to accompany my father to the center to find help for Elcy. I did everything they asked. The medium repeatedly waved his hands around my body, telling me to transfer positive energy. Soon my father began making frequent trips to the center and then demanded that all our family members participate in the sessions.

On one particular Thursday, amidst all of Elcy's agony, I went to the center to see if I could find a cure for myself. I had warts all over my body, from head to toe. I consulted a famous spiritualist doctor known as Dr. Santos Neto, who provided free care for the terminally ill. He looked me over from head to toe and went straight to the point:

"Which one is the biggest wart you have?"

"This one here," I said, pointing to my finger.

He reached for a fountain pen and drew a cross right on top of the wart and uttered an almost incomprehensible incantation.

"In a week, it will disappear. Believe me, boy."

Believe it or not, those warts disappeared seven days later! I was fascinated and believed even more in the healing power of the spiritist center. My body was cleansed. It was a sign, a supernatural indication that could put an end to my spiritual worries. Could it be that I had finally found God? A few weeks later, though, I looked in the mirror and saw a strange mark on my body—a wart had resurfaced. Days later, another one, and another, and another...

Later on, in the early days of the Universal Church, in our first headquarters church in the neighborhood of Abolição, I began noticing the manifestations of the spirits that cause illnesses in greater detail. The healing meetings were always full. I asked myself whether evil really had the power to heal—and if it did, how it used that power to keep us away from God, while granting the answer to our physical pain at the same time. I still see this happen often, even in supposedly Christian churches that claim to preach about Jesus.

In 1980, I wrote the book, *Orishas, Caboclos and Guides: Gods or Demons*[3], to relate my experiences in spiritual deliverance, even before I became a pastor. In one section I wrote about spiritual cures.

---

3 "Orixás, caboclos e guias: Deuses ou demônios?" A book explaining traditional occult practices in Brazil.

"The evil spirits do everything they can to attract and win over as many people as possible. In their demonic eagerness, they announce that they can heal, solve problems, bring wealth, free you of something or someone, help you realize your dreams, etc." The real truth about these alleged healings and invisible operations in spiritism is this: it's about taking control over a person.

Evil spirits come into them, and because these people do not have a strong Christian shield around them, the spirits cause sicknesses. Time passes and the spirits end up taking this person down a dark path, where these activities are practiced. The spirit causing the disease manifests in the medium, who then performs the supposed healing or operation. Or, the spirit can strike a deal with another evil spirit that is already dwelling in the medium. And so, the spirit leaves the person's body, and they become healed or "better."

When the spirits want to dominate someone's life by this method, they keep causing diseases to make the person suffer and then heal them afterwards, leaving the person almost completely well. I say "almost" because from this point on, their minds and hearts have been taken over by the "great work" that has supposedly occurred. That's how the spirits create problems in a person's life, and then sell them a quick and easy cure afterwards, just to bring back the problem once again in another way.

Many sick people who come to our meetings leave healed after we drive out all kinds of filthy spirits that inhabit them. Through the power of God, evil confesses its plans of destruction in the lives of those it possesses. All these things that I describe here are openly said by demons themselves when we exercise our faith in Jesus Christ and make them confess the truth about what they do.

Even going to the spiritist center did not cure Elcy's asthmatic bronchitis. Her respiratory crises usually kept her up all night long. But one early morning at dawn, after one of her exhausting episodes, she heard the radio message of a Canadian pastor on Mayrink Veiga, the famous station that had been first to broadcast the singer Carmen Miranda. Unable to sleep, she stayed up and listened to his entire sermon and prayed along with the pastor at the end.

She felt better right away. In the following days, Elcy listened intently to the radio program led by Robert McAlister, as he preached and invited listeners to worship at his New Life Church. Elcy accepted the invitation and decided to visit the place in downtown Rio.

Elcy's life turned around: her asthma disappeared and she faithfully attended that church. Her healing was so amazing that in less than a year, our whole family joined the newest follower of the gospel. I was the last one, but that didn't mean that I had lost interest in following God. My oldest sister's before-and-after story had woken me up. And though I never set foot in a Catholic church again after seeing that dead Jesus image, I still believed in my saints. I had faith. I was devoted to St. Joseph and always had a picture of him hanging around my neck. I carried the paper images of Joseph, Mary, and Jesus in my pocket or wallet. I still believed in my lucky charm—"God is great. Jesus Christ help me!"—whenever I felt scared. I believed that my illness had been healed at the spiritist center, even though it had come back even worse than before.

I was so uncertain. I didn't know what I wanted or what I should place my faith in.

As she became more dedicated to her new beliefs, Elcy began to speak regularly of the Bible at home. Her words touched me. I began trying to understand some passages of the Bible, but it was too hard to figure out. It all seemed so complicated. The symbolism, the names, expressions, and even the simplest spiritual messages were an indecipherable puzzle. It was all unfamiliar territory. Then I realized that I'd be able to understand more of the mysteries of the Bible if I attended the church services with my sister.

That was when I decided to go to New Life Church for the first time. From that day on, I went every Wednesday evening and Sunday morning, where around 500 would gather for the meetings. I was exactly 18 years old.

YOU MUST FORGIVE

I remained as an unconverted believer for more than a year, just attending the meetings with no commitment, with no encounter with God.

I tried to learn from the Bible teachings, but still kept the image of a saint in my pocket. I was in a phase of permanent fear. I worried about the future of my soul. The pastor preached salvation, but I would not surrender myself to God. I inwardly resisted, listening more to the voice in my heart than to the voice of reason.

The fate of my soul kept me awake. "If I die, where will I go?" I would ask myself at school, at work, or walking along the street. I was insecure because I was not sure of eternal life. Hell was imminent for me. During church services, whenever any of the pastors invited us to surrender our lives on the altar, I'd go straight up front.

"Who wants to accept Jesus as their only savior tonight?" I would always raise my hand.

"On this Sunday morning, who wants to accept the Lord Jesus as their savior?"

There I was with my hand raised. I don't even remember how many times I did this in one year. It happened so often that I lost count.

That was who I was when Ester first saw me at church, sitting in the balcony as usual. When we reminisce about those days, she tells me how sorry she had felt for me.

"One day I mentioned to my mother, 'Look at that poor guy. Every time the pastor asks, he accepts Jesus. He just doesn't get it, he never converts,'" she remembers.

Elcy, who was firm in her Christian faith, said I was very persistent and prayed a lot, but seemed lost.

Boy, was I lost.

I decided that I had to face my mess of a life head on. First, I'd have to bury my old self. I had to forgive.

I always had a bad temper. Forgiveness was not part of my character. I stopped talking to my sister Eris for two years. I was extremely temperamental and would get into fights for the most trivial reason. Proof of that is that I can't even remember why I had such hard feelings towards her. Even though I had become a churchgoer, I would stoke my resentment towards my own sister.

I tried to be friendly and open, so I made friends easily, but if someone did something against me, I'd fly into a rage and reject that person, and never want to have anything to do with them ever again. I would not forgive, period. The truth is that my feelings were pushed around by the devil,

I was disturbed and moody. Today I can say that openly, because I discovered what was within.

Forgiveness is one of the basic practices of the Christian faith. It's so important that Jesus said we should forgive not only seven times, but 70 times seven. Forgiveness must be infinite. The more we give, the more we receive. There are no limits to forgiveness.

I used to believe that time would erase my resentments, but it didn't. The pastor preached that it was necessary for me to forgive men in order for God to forgive me. "For if you forgive men their trespasses, your heavenly Father will also forgive you. But if you do not forgive men their trespasses, neither will your Father forgive your trespasses." (Matthew 6:14-15). I knew I'd have to put that hard lesson into practice. As John said, "He who is of God hears God's words" Inversely, whoever rejects the words of God, does not belong to God.

There was no other way. To find God, I would have to forgive. Unforgiveness nullified my prayers. Resentment literally closed the doors of heaven to my constant pleading every day. And so I went back to church and repeated the Lord's Prayer together with all the members. I spoke strong and determinedly.

"Forgive our sins, as we forgive those who sin against us," I proclaimed in chorus with the congregation, but it was just words, like the old saying, "do as I say, not as I do."

Forgiveness is a major obstacle for those who decide to convert to the Lord Jesus. During these past decades serving God at the altar, I have seen many people come to church, and yet die with hatred in their hearts—grudges against their father, son, wife or friend. The reasons are often trivial, but painful.

Forgiveness heals, sets free, and produces health and life. This is even proven medically. Forgiveness boosts the body's immunity against disease. Forgiveness frees the body of toxins that only do harm.

I have read several studies that show how resentment, placing blame, or holding grudges stimulates the release of stress hormones, which are harmful to the body when present over an extended period of time. Holding a grudge causes damage to the nervous system, the heart, and the immune system. Practicing forgiveness sets in motion positive responses to keep healthy, feel well, and control disease.

But how can we forgive? From the heart's point of view, it's humanly impossible. How can the heart be forced to stop feeling what it feels? It doesn't forget.

No human being is capable of controlling what the heart feels. The secret is to forgive with our mind. In our intellect and understanding, we have complete control. I decide to think, "Jesus tells me to forgive, for without forgiveness I will never reach Him. I want Jesus in my life, I want to forgive, so I choose to do so no matter what I feel."

I counsel people to act this way, solely through the inspiration of the Holy Spirit. I suggest a simple, straightforward prayer to those who cannot free themselves from unforgiveness: "I forgive this person in the name of Jesus. I want the Lord to bless them now."

Even if your heart feels something completely different, the fact that you pray to bless whoever hurt you can change everything. Even if you are too angry to mention the name of the person who offended you, God sees your effort and your intention to forgive, and with time, He'll remove the pain and heal the wounds of your heart. Without forgiveness, there is no salvation.

And so I continued to seek God at church with unforgiveness inside of me. The fear of hell would not let go.

Merely convinced

I had a busy life at that time. I'd have lunch in the Gloria district, then I'd leave for work at the lottery office in downtown Rio, and in the evenings I would study to prepare for university.

Since there was no direct transportation, I used to walk to work every day on my own, between 40 and 60 minutes.

That was my time for reflection. I would think about my life the future, and my aspirations. I would imagine my dreams with every step of that simple, routine walk. What 18-year-old doesn't have goals to accomplish, and dilemmas to solve? I still didn't know what kind of career to go for. Mathematics? Engineering? Economics? In what areas of exact sciences should I invest my knowledge?

I almost always thought about a career, what I would pursue in the future. But one day, as I was heading towards the Cinelandia region, a different thought popped into my head in the midst of the whirlwind of professional and financial projections I was making. I heard in my conscience a loud, clear voice that I had never heard before. A fixed idea in the form of a question, which was taken from the Word of God: "For what profit is it to a man if he gains the whole world, and loses his own soul?" (Matthew 16:26)

My fear of dying and going to hell increased after that day. I no longer slept in peace. At church, I'd raise my hand several times to accept Jesus because I would panic just at the thought of possibly losing salvation. Not for love and redemption, but solely because I wanted safety from hell. Jesus was not yet my Lord.

During that restless pursuit, I was baptized three times in water. Baptism by immersion symbolizes the burial of our sinful human character. It's a conscious act to completely kill our old earthly nature. Jesus explained the value of baptism and the new birth to an important Pharisee called Nicodemus: "...unless one is born of water and the Spirit, he cannot enter the kingdom of God." (John 3:5).

My first and second baptisms were worthless because I kept living that same old life. As long as I had doubts about my salvation, I'd keep getting baptized. There is only one true baptism. For my salvation, however, I was willing to be baptized a million times if necessary. Jesus was baptized by John the Baptist in Jordan River. He did not need to be, but He left us an example to follow.

I couldn't comprehend that the only way for baptism to be effective, was to start living according to the values of the Word of God. I would have to change completely, become different, be transformed into another being, be born again as another creature. It was necessary to live a new life. I would have to repent and abandon my sins once and for all. How could I be baptized in water without repenting from my sins?

The third baptism in water, a few years later, was the real one. But during that phase of frantically seeking God, I would be dunked into the baptistry a dry sinner and come back up a wet sinner, and nothing more. There was no change within. My attitudes were not mirroring what I claimed to believe in the church.

I was fostering uncertainty, and I lived in constant inner conflict, because I insisted on holding onto behavior that was incompatible with the Bible. My love life was a hot mess, with plenty of fooling around. Dating always ended up with something more than just dating. This is something I am definitely not proud of, because it held me back from finding God. I led a very immoral lifestyle. We have countless amazing testimonies of transformation in the Universal Church of people who had been living much like I did then, but back then my mistakes were adding up—and distancing me from God.

I continued to use the meetings at New Life Church to try and rid myself of hell. On Wednesdays or Sundays, my conscience was in pain, accusing me of my sins, and I would accept Jesus once more. I would sin outside the church, and then repeat the prayer before the pastor:

"Jesus have mercy on me, forgive me."

I was held hostage to this predicament. I had to either put up, or shut up. I was remorseful, but would not repent.

Remorse is not repentance. Remorse is but a momentary feeling of sadness for a wrong committed. Remorse does not choose to abandon sin, so there can be no forgiveness. Repentance is exactly the opposite. It's the attitude, action, and the practice of faith. Repenting lets go of sin, forever.

Theoretically, I appeared to be firm in my faith, but in practice, I was unchanged. There had been no transformation in my character or in my way of thinking or behavior. I had not been converted, I was only convinced of my faith.

This is one of the major ailments in Christian churches all over the world today, including the Universal Church, which creates a contingent of believers who have fallen and betrayed their faith within their churches and communities. Many of these believers are unfortunately, pastors, evangelists, apostles, bishops, and others with various titles and different positions.

There are believers who claim they believe in Jesus and the Bible, and are filled with the Holy Spirit, but are actually possessed by other spirits. The alarm was raised by the Lord Jesus Himself during the Sermon on the Mount: "Many will say to me on that day, 'Lord, Lord, did we not prophesy in your name and in your name drive out demons and in your name perform many miracles?' Then I will tell them plainly, 'I never knew you. Away from me, you evildoers!'" (Matthew 7:22-23).

This is very serious. This is a major warning sign to evangelical churches today. The current spiritual state of the Church is sorrowful. There are millions and millions of believers who have never become truly married to Jesus, people who have accepted Him many times, even followed a career in a religious institution, but have never truly surrendered themselves to Him.

They are like lovers having an affair. They meet secretly at night, and at times give in to their pleasure of a few hours, yet unwilling to make any commitment. They want to be free to enjoy their carnal desires. They claim they believe and think that's all they need. But when they're faced with struggles or adversity, they run to the church. And if they don't find an immediate way out of their problems, they'll run to a different denomination that suits them better. They're like birds that flit from tree to tree, looking for the answers they want.

Many of these types of believers have convinced themselves that they are already saved because they accepted Jesus in a prayer, but they are not. It is crucial that we surrender our lives with genuine faith. Giving up our own life for the Lord Jesus means a radical change of loyalties, a complete diversion from the path we once were on. It's true change.

They fooled me!

As the days unfolded at New Life Church, something started to change in me. I began to feel angry about how I had been fooled by idolatry for years. After one of my baptisms in water, I decided to destroy my images of saints and the medallion I wore around my neck. I placed them all on the floor and looked down on them with disgust, and let it all out:

"Bastards! You liars, you fooled me!" I shouted, stamping angrily on those pieces of paper and the necklace. I destroyed everything, without pity. Although I was not yet born of God, I began to despise all that wasted time I had spent, fooled by idolatry. I rebelled against the deceitfulness of Catholicism. One day, while I worked my shift as an office boy at the lottery, a priest came by. He was a leader from the Rio de Janeiro Archdiocese, and usually came to our office to receive financial grants that the government gave to certain Catholic societies at that time.

"Edir, a priest is heading to the board room. He didn't want to talk to me, wouldn't even look at my face, but "The Man," just told me he doesn't want anyone to walk in there without announcing him first," a colleague told me over the telephone. My colleague was a Christian who had left the Assemblies of God and worked at reception.

My desk was in a large room on the third floor of the building. The boardroom was on the fourth floor, where "The Man"—the head of the lottery department, director-secretary doctor Paulo Vidal Leite Ribeiro, a war veteran—was working.

The priest was in fact a monsignor. He rushed up the stairs. I had barely put the telephone down before he appeared, grumpy and thin, and almost ran me over. I stopped in front of him and said:

"Sir, please allow me to announce you to our director! Whom shall I say is here?"

He stopped and gave me a nasty stare. He measured me up with an angry look. Who does this kid think he is to stop me?

"Paulo is waiting for me, young man," he replied.

Then he stepped to the right to pass by me. I also stepped quickly to the right and again stopped in front of him. The look on the monsignor's face grew more furious. He breathed heavily. He saw I was not going to let him go up without authorization from my boss.

Please have a seat while I go upstairs to let him know you're here," I told him fearlessly.

"He's expecting me, kid."

"But you may not enter without the announcement of your arrival. I have orders."

The monsignor glared at me furiously, but did not move a step. It became clear that I wouldn't budge. While I prepared to go up to the boardroom, he turned his back, and stormed out of the building.

After half an hour, Doctor Paulo's secretary called me upstairs. I walked in to his office, head bowed but confident that I had done the right thing. He stuttered with rage, barely able to bawl me out the way he wanted to

"Wh... wh... wh... what in the world have you done? Th... th... th... th... that's the envoy of the archbishop of all people!"

"I was just following orders, Doctor Paulo," I replied.

I'm sure I wasn't fired only because I worked for the government. The Catholic Church was on my blacklist from that day on, and symbolically, that would be a sign of what would become the burden of the Universal Church throughout the years. Thanks to the instruction from the Holy Spirit, millions of people all over the world have been released from the blindness of idolatry and religious slavery through the power of the gospel that my companions and I have preached from the pulpit.

But that was not the reason I eventually surrendered my life to do the work of God on the altar. What motivated me to preach the Word of God was obedience to an explicit commandment of Jesus: "Go into all the world and preach the gospel to every creature. He who believes and is baptized will be saved; but he who does not believe will be condemned."

(Mark 16:15-16). My greatest revolt was not against idolatry, but against the fact that so many people did not know the Lord Jesus Christ. It was the same situation I had experienced those first years attending New Life Church.

As I approached 19 years of age and got more involved with a life of faith, I also made another decision. Though I still hadn't found God yet, I was aware of right and wrong in all aspects of life. The pastor preached very clearly about the importance of tithing in the work of God, but I never valued it much until the day I chose to do something about it.

In early December 1965, I decided I would give my tithes. I wanted to take my faith seriously. So, in January 1966, I paid my first tithe, and I have never stopped. This faithfulness has stuck with me to this day. I usually say during my meetings, that the moment we hand over our tithes and offerings, we honor the Lord God. Exactly: an honor. That's how we consider the act of faithful tithing and the giving of offerings.

A tithe is not an offering. Tithes are the first fruits of a harvest, returned to the Lord of the earth. Today, in practice, it's the first ten percent of all we earn or bring in financially. Tithes signify the loyalty of a servant to his Lord. The Creator needs nothing from the creation, but has instituted the law of tithes and offerings to test the faithfulness and love of His servants.

Only those who are servants take the commandments of the Lord to heart and practice them. Those who do not serve by honoring Him this way, according to what we read in His Word, He views as thieves.

I went to personally check what was written in the scriptures. My duty was explicit and clear, as well as my rights: "Yet from the days of your fathers You have gone away from My ordinances and have not kept them. Return to Me, and I will return to you, says the Lord of hosts. But you said, 'In what way shall we return?' Will a man rob God? Yet you have robbed Me! But you say, 'In what way have we robbed You?' In tithes and offerings. You are cursed with a curse, for you have robbed Me, even this whole nation. Bring all the tithes into the storehouse, that there may be food in My house, and try Me now in this, says the Lord of hosts, If I will not open for you the windows of heaven and pour out for you such blessing that there will not be room enough to receive it. And I will rebuke the devourer for your sakes, so that he will not destroy the fruit of your ground, nor shall the vine fail to bear fruit for you in the field, says the Lord of hosts. And all nations will call you blessed. For you will be a delightful land, says the Lord of hosts." (Malachi 3:7-12).

I knew that the act of returning to the Lord should start with faithfulness in my tithes. This was the condition God established with His people in the past, and in my case, it couldn't be any different.

For Him to grant me favor, I should obey His Word. I also learned, that when we "devour" the tithes that belong to the Lord, we are in fact turning our backs on our own lives. That's why, as an example, many nations suffer with the most horrific losses of all kinds. It may seem simplistic to believe that the act of robbing God of tithes and offerings

The great day

I was with a girl who I liked a lot, but who did not accept the changes that started happening in me. She thought that church was boring, and that Christian commitments were a waste for people our age. Her goal in life was to make the most of having fun, to indulge her desires and to be free to pursue her dreams as much as she wanted.

Our two-year relationship ended when she broke up with me. I was deeply in love. We had no rules and lived our lives as if we were married, and she eventually tired of our love life. I also had my uncertainties. I wished she would join me in church, but she did only two or three times.

I was so madly in love that I actually begged God with a good deal of disrespect and immaturity:

"God, if you love Jesus, bring her back to me."

I pleaded in vain. In the next book in this series, I describe in detail how I was fooled by the passions of my heart when I stopped using intelligent faith.

It was because of these unhealthy desires that I was unable to have a stable relationship with God. I became depressed and inconsolable. I suffered greatly and held on to faith even harder. Pushed by the disappointment and the bitterness of rejection, I ran to Jesus. Wounded, I was ready to make the most important decision of my life.

I was feeling sad, with my head bowed, as I heard yet another altar call from the pastor at the meeting:

"Is anyone not sure of their salvation and wants that assurance now?"

Again, I stood up with my hand raised. But this time I was different. Moved by pain, I didn't care about anything else. I spoke with the deepest sincerity from my soul, and ripped open my deepest feelings from head to toe to pour them out to God. I could no longer take living under the fear of hell. I wanted to give myself one hundred percent, with every ounce of my being.

I had nothing else to lose.

"Lord! Lord! Give me the assurance of salvation!" I said so strongly that it seemed like the words were being ripped out of my chest.

Two weeks later, I attended another meeting on my own. There were no friends or relatives there. The pastor once again told me to stand up. Eyes closed. Spirit redeemed.

The hymn was a song in the form of a prayer:

Oh, how blind I have walked and lost I have wandered, far, far from my Savior.
But from the heavens He came, and his blood poured out, to save a sinner such as I.

At the cross, at the cross, where I saw my sin being punished in Jesus...[4]

The words were powerful. I saw my sins. Though I didn't consider myself to be a big sinner, I recognized I was someone who had lived life the wrong way, and I bowed. I saw I was a sinner full of doubts. My debts were unpayable. Each word was a jab to my mind, a stab in my spirit.

I didn't think my life had been so bad. I had no addictions, didn't steal, didn't murder. Deep inside, submerged in my pit of pride, I hadn't considered myself a sinner who deserved hell. The hymn was still being sung in the background stirring me to take a good hard look at the state of my life. I thought about my real condition as a sinner, something that brought despair, pain, and horror.

The Holy Spirit convicted me of my countless faults, an experience that turned me into the smallest of creatures, the most insignificant of men, dirt to be tossed into the gutter.

...It was there by faith, I received my sight and now I am happy in Your light.
I used to hear about such matchless grace,
which from the heavens brought us Jesus.
But I turned a deaf ear, did not want to convert to the Lord,
who died on the cross for me...[5]

4 *"Oh quão cego andei e perdido vaguei,/ longe, longe do meu Salvador./ Mas do céu ele desceu, e seu sangue verteu,/ para salvar a um tão pobre pecador./ Foi na cruz, foi na cruz, onde um dia eu vi/ meu pecado castigado em Jesus..."*

5 *"...Foi ali, pela fé, que os olhos abri/ e agora me alegro em Sua luz. / Eu ouvia falar dessa graça sem par,/ que do céu trouxe que por mim morreu na cruz..."*

This time, the song blended with my prayer. I plead honestly for God to forgive me:

"My God, I want to change. I don't want to be like this any more. Help me!"

...but one day I felt my sin
and above me saw the sword of the law.
I fled in haste, in Jesus I hid
and safe shelter I found with Him...[6]

That very moment, tears poured from my eyes.

I ran to God because I was suffering. I was groaning in pain, wounded and begging for relief. I had seen my sin and tried to run, but the ground fell out from under me. Who could save me? The Holy Spirit convicted me of my sins. I saw myself lost in an endless inferno. I screamed for help. Who could save me? And that same spirit, the Holy Spirit, pointed to the only One able to reach me: The Lord Jesus Christ.

So I ran to Jesus. Through faith, I cast my body, soul, and spirit into His hands.

I was flooded with indescribable peace, followed by a joy that's impossible to explain. I will never forget those moments, nor can I describe precisely how they happened.

While I was singing and praying, my body was soaked with sweat.

...How fortunate, then, is this heart of mine,
finding such excellent love.

6 *"...Mas um dia senti meu pecado/ e vi sobre mim a espada da lei./ Apressado fugi, em Jesus me escondi,/ e abrigo seguro Nele achei..."*

That led Jesus to suffer at the cross,
to save a sinner such as I...[7]

The tune went on playing, the sound I needed to hear. It was really at the cross that I saw my mistakes. His sacrifice on Calvary made me aware of my total insignificance.

At that moment, I loved Jesus. The greatest of all treasures. A priceless gem. Unequaled riches.

The Holy Spirit revealed the Lord Jesus to me. I had found my God.

...It was on the cross, on the cross, where I saw my sin being punished in Jesus... [8]

---

7 *"...Quão ditoso, então, este meu coração,/ conhecendo o excelso amor./ Que levou meu Jesus a sofrer lá na cruz,/ pra salvar a um tão pobre pecador..."*

8 *"...Foi na cruz, foi na cruz,/ onde um dia eu vi meu pecado castigado em Jesus..."*

I HAD DEMONS

I left the meeting walking on air. It's impossible to describe the feeling: peace, safety, trust, joy. Even if I lived to be 200, I would never forget a single detail of that incomparable experience of fulfillment. Something incredible happened to me, as if a light had shone throughout my whole body, I was no longer in darkness. God had set me free.

My eyes and my ears had been opened. Now I could worship God and hear and understand His Word. I felt like laughing and weeping all at the same time. My soul was light; gone was the weight of hell. I felt like the Greeks must have felt when they ascended the mountains to Jerusalem during the feast of the Passover to learn what they still did not know, despite all of their philosophy and advanced knowledge of the time. Jesus stated: "The hour has come for the Son of Man to be glorified." (John 12:23)

The Greeks wanted to meet the Son of God in the midst of one of the holiest of traditional Jewish ceremonies, which caused them to change their focus from the feast in Jerusalem to the Kingdom of Heaven. *"I tell you, in the same way, there will be more joy in heaven over one sinner who repents than over ninety-nine righteous people who don't need repentance."* (Luke 15:7).

That same feast happened on the day of my new birth. God transformed my cry of agony into a cry of happiness. I no longer missed my ex-girlfriend. The feeling I had for her had faded and was replaced by another one with greater impact and of immense benefit to me. "Hallelujah, I can finally talk about something I've learned on my own. I know what I am talking about. I've experienced this wonder," I thought, smiling to myself.

It was a personal experience, my private moment with God. The change took place from the inside out. I was reborn a new creature. From then on, at every meeting, I no longer raised my hand to accept Jesus. I made the most of the moments of prayer to surrender myself to God even more. I sought the Lord God with a staunch will. Praise, obedience, attention to His heavenly will, and tears of purity became part of my routine at our meetings.

I'd barely leave the service and I'd already be counting the minutes when I could go back to church again, motivated by a growing desire to understand the thoughts of God more deeply. My face was glowing. The sons of Israel saw the face of Moses shine when he climbed down Mount Sinai with the Ten Commandments; the rescuer of Israel had seen God. No one is the same after seeing Him face to face.

Upon leaving the service that day, I was overwhelmed with such uncontrollable pleasure that I wanted to hug everyone. I wanted to hug whoever I saw in front of me: the church members heading home, pedestrians, beggars on the side of the road. "Thank You, my Lord! I've found You! Thank You, thank You!" I thought those words on my way home. I was just expressing my gratitude for having lived through the most extraordinary experience in this life. I clearly understood that I would never find a greater treasure for the rest of my days.

The day after that unforgettable meeting, on the way to work at the lottery, I met a beggar on a street. He was propped up against the wall as he lay on the sidewalk, shivering while many pedestrians passed him by as if he were invisible. I stopped walking, looked at that sight, and had an uncontrollable yearning to help that man.

"Here, take my coat, sir."

He looked at me, took the coat, and said nothing.

I went on my way. I started to love people with a love that was not mine.

I had in fact, turned into light. The demons that had inhabited my body had been ripped out. Though I had never manifested evil spirits before, I had had demons. That's right, there had been evil spiritual forces controlling my being and my way of thinking. I had been involved with other beliefs. I had turned my back on the teachings of God.

Though I never manifested those entities in church, I had lived under their dominion. I suffered like a puppet in the grip of hell just like so many who attend our Universal Church chains if prayer for deliverance on a daily basis. These people are only set free from the influence of these spirits after these demons, who mistreat them so violently, manifest and are cast out. I had been set free by the Word. I listened to the guidance of the Holy Spirit, and what Jesus had spoken and determined was passed on to me: "You are already clean because of the word I have spoken to you" (John 15:3). His promise came true with me.

My encounter with God caused a full transformation in my character. I was no longer anxious or moody, nor did I get offended by word or behavior that I didn't like. I learned to turn the other cheek. I forgave my sister, and we started treating each other as siblings. I held no grudge against her, and my forgiveness was real. That selfish, egotistical, resentful, and moody personality had been buried.

Little by little, I left behind my worldly friends. I gave up on friends who contributed nothing to my spiritual growth. Most of the time they'd either steer me away from Christian principles or try to lead me back to my old habits. I felt I had no choice but to isolate myself and run away from sin. I knew that now I was permanently in the crosshairs of the devil. It was crucial for me to keep my eyes wide open.

I radically changed how I managed my love life. The pain of losing my ex-girlfriend disappeared at last and was replaced by a constant thought that there was something greater reserved for me. My future would be promising if I persisted in following the steps of Jesus.

I had other girlfriends at that time, but I didn't feel sure about any of them. I dreamed of married life, as a family man, happy with a woman of God by my side who I would truly love. But the examples and stories that surrounded me made me cautious. None of my siblings had a happy marriage. I was witness to a lot of fighting among couples in our family. Fearful, I prayed to God, asking that He would spare me from a failed, unhappy marriage.

Even at home I was misunderstood. Seeing me single, seeking God, and increasingly involved with the things of faith, my mother would say:

"Edir, dear, you have to go out and date. You have to marry."

I would thank her for her love and care, but I had chosen a goal. I did not want to displease my God, in spite of my imperfections and limitations. I left behind the old friends I used to hang around with. I no longer went clubbing, or to parties and fun fairs with no constraints, places where I had spent the nights dancing without even bothering to feel tired. I tried to avoid anything that would even hint at grieving God.

I spent Saturday nights, single and alone, while everyone else was out having fun with girl or boyfriends, and the lonely would go out searching for company. At that time there were no church services on Saturday nights. It was only open on Wednesdays and Sundays. Nowadays, the Universal Church opens its doors every day of the week and dedicates Thursdays to those who are searching for a partner in their romantic lives, as I used to do in those times. I consider our Love Therapy sessions on Thursdays to be one of the most important aspects of our spiritual work. It has helped thousands of couples and single people all over the world, find happiness in married life together, based on Christian principles.

On those Saturday nights in the years after my conversion, I used to close myself up in my bedroom alone and talk to God. Jesus had given that instruction: "But you, when you pray, go into your room, and when you have shut your door, pray to your Father who is in the secret place; and your Father who sees in secret will reward you openly." (Matthew 6:6).

There, in the solitude of my room, I meditated on the scriptures and prayed for hours on end. I even read the entire Bible. I would meditate on four or five chapters each day. I gave myself to God in prayer, in moments of unconditional intimacy. When there were people at home, I would pray in a low voice. When I was alone, I would raise my voice. I would plead and seek with an unexplained pleasure in my soul that would often lead me to sing and dance in the presence of God.

What splendid moments!

Those simple times strengthened me and provided me with new experiences on this path of faith. One day, when thinking about how amazing the events of the Bible were, an excerpt about David's heroic triumph popped into my mind: "For who is this uncircumcised Philistine, that he should defy the armies of the living God?" (1 Samuel 17:26).

Although I was young and could not even imagine all the signs and wonders God would put into my life in the future, David's question caused a sense of revolt in me. It produced an explosion of certainty and contentment in my being. I leapt in my room. I had a short vision of the moments in years to come when we would challenge and knock down so many Goliaths, and many others that we still have yet to knock down.

My change in behavior also produced some stressful situations. In my job at the lottery office, I told my colleagues that I had found God and would routinely be the target of teasing. My colleagues would try to tempt me by showing me porn from men's magazines. One day, a female co-worker spread out a poster of a naked woman on my desk.

"Take a look, if you're a real man," she said, as everyone laughed.

After that happened I locked myself in the bathroom to pray.

I wept a lot in the bathroom at work. My colleagues eyed me with discrimination and disdain. I had no choice but to stay away from those old friends. I would try to keep to myself in my corner. No one had anything to offer me. It was important not to be influenced to veer from the path I had decided to follow. Those who claim to follow Jesus, but stay involved in friendships that are contrary to faith, hardly ever resist. They cave in to the first temptation. And I could not cave in.

THE EDGE OF THE KNIFE

Another natural characteristic of the beginning of my journey, was my spiritual immaturity. In my naïvete as a neophyte, a name used in the gospels for those new in the faith, I committed common mistakes and slip-ups that time taught me to overcome. As with everything in life, time is an essential ally to build our relationship with God.

It's interesting to see that not even the Holy Spirit is able to make us grow if we do not subject ourselves to the lessons of time. It's necessary to experience problems so that we learn how to overcome certain situations. Tribulations are all a part of the teaching process of the Spirit of God. When we are led to moments that corner us in a maze of doubt and fear, it's faith in the promise of the Lord Jesus that rejuvenates us: "And surely I am with you always, to the very end of the age" (Matthew 28:20). And so from weakness we extract strength.

Before talking more about this, let me share what happened to me during that early period after my conversion.

First, I developed ta peculiar trait of all Christians who are new to the faith: I started to talk about Jesus all the time, at any opportunity, and to anyone indiscriminately. At work, on the bus, in the street, and at school. I had neither the control nor the wisdom to be considerate.

I became a real bore. A complete bore. I turned into a kind of "Jesus freak," which kept other people from noticing my transformation and instead saw only what appeared to be fanaticism.

Every day, I would witness to one of my classmates at the university preparation course. I couldn't even pay attention to studying because I was so anxious to win that friend over to Jesus. I'd talk and repeat myself so much that he could barely look at me. After some time, he'd head off in another direction when he saw me coming, just to avoid having to listen to me. One day, he interrupted me even before I started talking.

"Listen, Edir, everyone has their own religion. You follow yours and I follow mine," he cut me short. "I'm here to study, and I have to concentrate on that. Sorry, okay..."

Silenced and feeling awkward, I slunk into my chair and hid in the classroom. But the disappointment was so great that I could hardly concentrate on the class.

After converting, I thought everyone would be open and totally receptive to the message of salvation. I thought everyone would want to hear about my amazing experience. How childish I was in the faith! I didn't realize that people's rejection of the gospel was because evil spirits were running interference in their minds, which is why they reacted negatively to my testimony of transformation.

Later on, I learned that not everyone is willing to hear about the Kingdom of God and that if we keep insisting we risk throwing our pearls to the swine. Jesus taught: "Do not give what is holy to the dogs; nor cast your pearls before swine, lest they trample them under their feet, and turn and tear you in pieces." (Matthew 7:6)

We must always be discerning and take the opportunities the Holy Spirit gives us. He knows about our deep desire to help. Often, those who are suffering come to us themselves, and so the right moment to witness the power of God and talk about our personal experience appears. Otherwise, by opening ourselves up without wisdom, we can appear to be radicals, which may actually alienate people rather than bring them closer to God. We evangelize with words accompanied by our behavior. I repeat that all the time to the pastors I meet on my missionary travels. Our life must show the real difference that the power of God creates. Jesus Himself said that, "I was sent only to the lost sheep of Israel." We must seek the lost, the sick, the prisoners, the hungry, and those who are suffering and mistreated in general. Jesus can only save those who are lost.

How then do we rescue those who don't think they're lost?

My classmate's negative response was a strong blow for me. But my attitude was sincere. On the way back home, along Franklin Roosevelt Avenue in downtown Rio, alone and on foot, in the darkness of the Flamengo landfill, I wept. I wept so strong that I was sobbing. In a low voice, I asked myself, and God at the same time:

"I told him about saving his soul and what did I get for an answer?"

My Father, all I wanted was to win that guy over to Jesus.

I didn't know it, but at that moment God heard my prayer and saw my sincere intention to win souls. Looking back, I see that the Bible is true: "Those who sow in tears shall reap in joy. He who continually goes forth weeping, bearing seed for sowing, shall doubtless come again with rejoicing, bringing his sheaves with him." (Psalm 126:5-6).

Over the years, I have learned to develop a balance when it comes to faith. I have grasped that I should counterbalance in a variety of ways. Every creation has a point of balance. The human body, a vehicle, an aircraft—everything works within balance. In the world of faith, it's no different.

Many converts have become frustrated because they overdo it when making decisions of faith. They interpret the teachings of the Word of God, seeing and judging situations, in a hypercritical way. Everything is judged by the edge of the knife, precisely the opposite of King Solomon's lesson, one of the wisest men in the history of humanity: "Do not be overly righteous, nor be overly wise: Why should you destroy yourself?" (Ecclesiastes 7:16)

During these years in charge of the work of God, I have witnessed some unbalanced cases of faith put into practice, due to an exaggerated concept of righteousness. For example, some church members will tithe on their income down to the last cent, meticulous to follow the letter of the law. I am obviously not criticizing their loyalty in paying their tithes, but their extreme self-righteous attitude while doing so.

For those types of Christians, the most innocent small talk is viewed as scandalous. The majority of them forget that though they don't belong to the world, they still do live in it. What's worse is that many abandon Jesus for not managing to meet their own extremely high standards. They just burn out and give up. Balancing our faith does not mean we tolerate sin, yet we don't overdo being holy either.

So with time, I came to understand that even after my new birth, I would still never be perfect. It's impossible. I am a human being. Even filled with the Spirit of God, I am still "this treasure in jars of clay to show that this all-surpassing power is from God and not from us" (2 Corinthians 4:7).

And for many people, there lies the mistake. They think that communion with God is an assurance that they will be perfect. Our new hearts that will be made perfect, according to God. Our mind will be perfect once it is shaped by the thoughts of God. But we will be subject to failures because we are human beings, because we inhabit this world and are subject to its fallen state.

Finding Jesus changed my life, but of course I have not become perfect. In these 48 years serving God, I have failed many times. I was no saint. Like anyone else, I have my day-to-day problems and trials, and I often make mistakes. God allows this so that the mistakes serve as lessons. I have learned a lot in this time. I have understood, for example, that tribulations build our foundations of faith. I have discovered that the more struggles, the more adversities, and the firmer we hold to our convictions, the humbler we become before God. In anguish, we obtain maturity.

Experience has made me unshaken by events I would never have imagined witnessing inside the church. Since becoming born again, nothing shakes me any more. While I was still crawling as a baby in faith at New Life Church, I saw pastors committing adultery, fights between pastors, accidents, diseases and various tragedies. One pastor who I liked very much was killed in a car accident. Some of Bishop Robert McAlister's dissenters stole a radio station he had purchased, taking advantage of the fact that he was a foreigner. I witnessed some of the most egregious political issues at the church. I always stayed silent and never got involved in any of it, but I did not feel shaken. I would only pray and ask God for protection for His work.

I firmly and faithfully followed the direction of the gospel, but there was still something missing. At services, I would always check the sermon notes with the Bible. I was especially watchful of what the servants of God were teaching about the Holy Spirit, the Breath of God, the third person of the Holy Trinity. God the Father, God the Son and God the Holy Spirit. The mantle of power that could dwell inside of us.

Questions would cross my mind. What is this gift of God and why is it said to be so important? How does this miracle work? What does it mean and how would this affect me? I've found God, but do I have to struggle once more to be baptized in the Holy Spirit? How will He indwell me? Do I have what it takes to receive such a gift? Who was I for this to live in me?

I soon set off to find my newest treasure.

My daughter Viviane's birth defect brought great suffering. She required a number of surgeries to her face and needed various medications and therapies. But it was what I needed to turn around my life through faith.

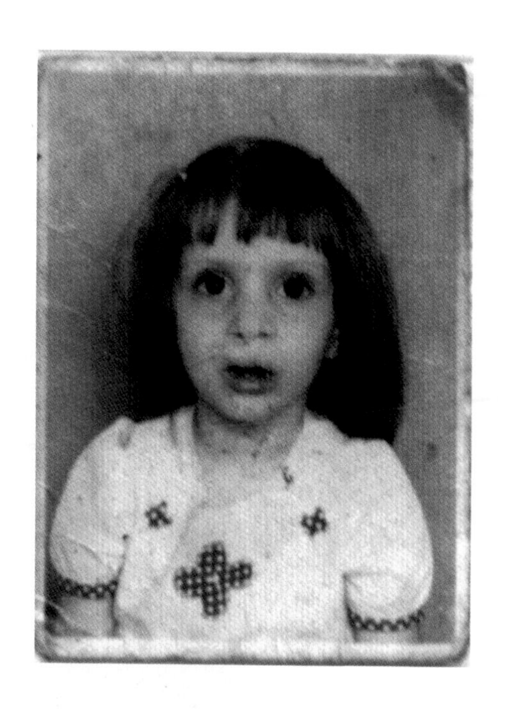

Cristiane and Viviane have always been very close sisters, ever since they were young.

Despite trauma and insecurity, both had a stable childhood. Cristiane grew to be her younger sister's guardian.

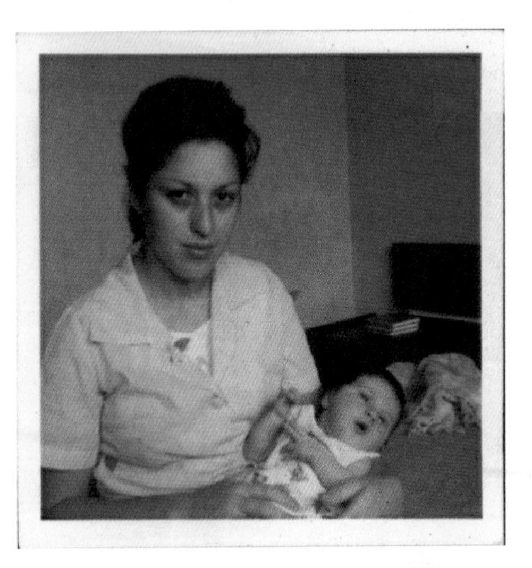

Cristiane at birth on her mother's lap, and slightly older in my arms. (left) Smiling at her two-year old birthday party.

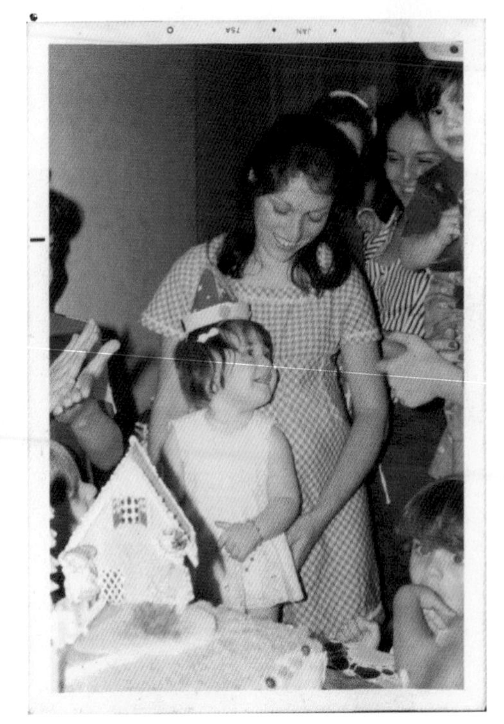

Ester was always a provider of advice and firmness in their development.

When our daughters were still in their adolescent years, we adopted Moses, another dear child. The years we lived abroad brought our family even closer.

A sacred moment: mealtime at our home with Ester and Moses.

Viviane and Cristiane as teenagers.

When they were young, Cristiane and Viviane mirrored their mother's behavior and character.

Our family nowadays in the rare moments that we manage to get together.
My daughters and I dedicate our lives entirely to the Work of God.

A special service in Rio de Janeiro to celebrate the 50th anniversary of my parent's marriage.

During the service, I asked my siblings, cousins, nephews and nieces to come to the altar and thank God for my parents' lives.

Dona Geninha with grand-daughter Cristiane. Her love for the children also helped us in the struggle against Viviane's illness.

My six siblings together to celebrate our mother's birthday in the city of Simão Pereira.

Aqui está seu lindo
filho trabalhando na neve
Quem podia imaginar isso!
Como as cousas mudam, não?
No próximo inverno espero
que esteja conosco para ver a
neve, como é bonita!
Beijos,
Ester
New York, Feb 1987

The sweet post-cards Ester sent my mother in February, 1987 when we moved to New York, United States.

Para minha querida
sogra, uma lembrança de
seus filhos que tanto lhe
amam e lhe apreciam.
Beijos,
Ester
New York, Feb 1937

In April, 1997, eight months before she passed away, I wrote her a card to acknowledge all she did for me and our family.

São Paulo, 8/4/97

Mamãe:

Eu louvo e agradeço a Deus pela senhora. Nunca esqueci suas lutas por cada um de nós!

Que Deus a abençoe abundantemente!

Going against everyone and everything, dona Geninha always believed that I would achieve my dream of preaching the Word of God.

In pursuit of a new miracle

To find God, I found out that it was necessary to establish priorities in faith. I had to define what I wanted. This formula would be repeated in my pursuit of the Holy Spirit. I had countless goals that I wanted to reach. I had many dreams, but I had to decide which one was more important. I wanted to grow professionally, make money, find a wife, raise a family, and be happy, but I had to put the Holy Spirit in first place.

I started to pray and ask God for that gift, and meditated on the Bible, focusing on a greater knowledge of the Holy Spirit. I read over and over the verses that dealt with that baptism from heaven. I would underline passages once or twice and meditate on them several times every day. Whenever possible, I thought about the Holy Spirit—on the street, at home, at work, anywhere. In everything I did, I concentrated on the same objective: "I desire the Lord, Holy Spirit, in my body, soul, and spirit, with all the strength of my understanding."

I was living in that belief as if it were on the eve of my wedding day. I make use of this easy example in my preaching now. I say we should look at the receiving God's Spirit as a marriage, one of the most important moments in our lives. A few weeks before the wedding, a couple doesn't think about anything other than the dress, the suit, the clothes for the best men and bridesmaids, the invitations, the ceremony, the guest list, the decorations, the reception, the cake. No detail can be overlooked. Up until that great day, the couple lives are totally absorbed in the wedding.

Marriage to the Holy Spirit is no different. In order to receive Him, a believer must fill his or her thoughts with Him, up to the moment of receiving His indwelling. That is the main secret. The Holy Spirit does not just come into the lives of human beings in a casual way. He comes when there is total surrender, an earnest effort seek him, and a clear demonstration of a willingness to pay the price to receive Him. This happens when faith is joined by action.

One of the passages of the Bible that touched me the most was the strong warning of Paul to the Romans. I meditated on it for several weeks with fear and trembling: "Now if anyone does not have the Spirit of Christ, he is not His." (Romans 8:9). If I wanted to belong to the Lord Jesus, I had to have His Spirit.

I was trying to create a new mind, but it was not easy.

I followed some fundamental steps to receive the Holy Spirit. The first was to realize that no one received the baptism because they deserved it. I didn't deserve it and could never imagine that I did. I should yearn and struggle for this baptism with all my heart by faith in the Lord Jesus.

He had promised, so even though I was undeserving, I had the right to receive Him through faith in His promise.

The second step, which I had already begun, was desire. It couldn't just be a simple wish, but a desire much like the aching and longing for the forgiveness of our sins. It's a burning want, greater than any other dream or desire of the heart—more than living, getting married, gaining wealth or possessions, more than anything this world has to offer.

The third step was to keep my thoughts constantly centered on the Holy Spirit. To do so, I had to isolate myself from everything that was harmful to a good conscience. I avoided bad company, daily distractions, and even apparently mundane activities that could interrupt my relationship with the Spirit.

It was no easy task to take control of my mind. I was subject to constant attacks of evil with a string of dirty, corrupt thoughts. Demonic thoughts related to God and sex, for example. And due to pure inexperience, these thoughts disturbed me greatly. I even thought I was sinning against the Holy Spirit, and for that reason, would never be able to receive Him.

I found my pastor and explained what I was going through without going into detail. He prayed for me and I was set free from those thoughts. But after some time, the same filthy ideas invaded my mind once more. This time, I was alone and I had to learn to react with my own faith.

I decided to speak to the devil himself.

"Listen, Satan! From now on, whenever you bring this trash to my mind, I'm just going to worship and glorify my Lord!" I said with determination.

I acted this way because I remembered that the devil hates to see us worshipping God. Every time those thoughts would pop into my mind, I would react with praise to my Lord. I praised Jesus and soon I no longer thought about those things. I resisted evil and it ran away from me.

After that day, I was free from that torment. I always repeat the same strategy whenever my mind is attacked with filth. I didn't falter in my counterattack to against those thoughts. I also refused to believe that I had sinned against God. Being tempted is not a sin, it is only sinful to give in to temptation.

It was the sign that I was on the right path to receive the Holy Ghost.

The miracle happened two years after my encounter with God. I was about to turn 21. The first evidence of my baptism was an unexpected reaction during a prayer vigil during a special seven-day campaign to receive the Holy Spirit. That was rare because the New Life Church was only open a few days a week. The meeting days were limited, which kept me from giving myself to serving God even more.

On that day, I spoke in tongues, which, according to the Bible, is one of the signs of receiving the Spirit of God. I spoke just one single word and became suspicious. I thought I might simply be imitating the pastor who was saying incomprehensible things during the service on the altar. I did not speak that word again for some time. I was not anxious or worried about receiving the Holy Spirit. I also didn't have a good understanding of the dimension or of the invaluable importance of baptism, as we so often teach in our current preachings.

After a few months, on a Sunday morning, the late Pastor Otavio Peterson, took an innovative turn during the service. He asked for all present to place their hands on the person sitting in front of them.

"Now, each one is to pray for the other. Ask God to visit us with His Holy Spirit," the pastor instructed over the microphone.

I was in the last row, and there was no one to place their hand on my head. I obeyed his instructions. When I started praying for the person in front of me, my words immediately began to sound strange. From then on, I started to speak in tongues. The interesting thing is that, at the time, a strong certainty came over me that the Holy Spirit was with me. There was no laughter, crying, or emotional excess. Only certainty. I didn't fall on the floor, roll around, feel chills, start spinning, or go into spasms. It was a moment of absolute awareness. I knew exactly what was going on.

From then on, a sense of perfect peace overcame me, not only at church, but also with my relatives, friends, and in my daily life. As a consequence of that baptism, the fruit of the Spirit of God was born in me. Nine qualities, each one described by the Apostle Paul: "But the fruit of the Spirit is love, joy, peace, longsuffering, kindness, goodness, faithfulness, gentleness, self-control." (Galatians 5:22-23). The Bible says "the fruit is," not "the fruits are." It's not grammatical carelessness, but a teaching for life: the fruit is a composition of nine equally essential parts for Christians. As soon as such spiritual unity is reached, there is boldness, faith, and trust.

As it happened in the upper room on Mount Zion in Jerusalem on that memorable day of Pentecost, the Spirit of God descended in power into my life. I was sealed to receive guidance and inspiration. It is He who exhorts me, advises me, comforts me, renews me and uplifts me in the wars I fight against hell then and now.

He is the mentor of the Universal Church of the Kingdom of God. Without the Holy Spirit, nothing that has been done would be possible. I admit that without Him the UCKG and I would not exist. I would be nothing.

Nothing.

A DREAM OF PAIN

Giving birth can take hours. The pain felt when a baby comes into the world varies among women and even from one pregnancy to another. But physicians generally consider it one of the worst pains felt by the human body.

There's the extra weight bearing down on the belly and back. The labor pains begin lightly and gradually increase. The belly hardens, like a wall. In the beginning, the pain is less, but is already disturbing. Some women take a walk or stay immersed in water in an attempt to relieve the pressure, but to no avail. The pressure on the back is strong due to the baby's movement. When the contractions increase, the feeling is like everything inside is bursting. There are a few minutes of relief, and the next contraction starts soon after.

The intervals between contractions shorten as the baby arrives. Contractions happen every minute, and the intensity of the pain increases. When the moment comes to push the child out of the mother's body, the pain reaches its peak. Many women have never done such hard work in their lives. At the moment of birth, the woman contorts herself, holds tight to the bed or someone's arm, screams, or clenches a towel between her teeth. The pain is incomparable to any other. For some, it is the most intense pain that exists.

Even as a man, I can perceive how strong that pain is. It is the same pain that the Apostle Paul wrote about to the Christians in Galatia: "My little children, for whom I labor in birth again until Christ is formed in you." (Galatians 4:19).

Those pains appeared from the beginning of my path to faith. I had been born again, found God, and received the baptism in the Holy Spirit, but something more was missing. A fire, a flaming eruption started to burn out of control within me, to the point of placing me in unbelievable situations for those who have never gone through the "pains of childbirth."

My projections for the future had dwindled, of my own accord. I had lost all motivation to pursue a career and become financially successful, as none of that fulfilled me any more. My recent enrollment in the mathematics program at Santa Úrsula University no longer excited me. I only stayed one-and-a-half years and requested a transfer to the Federal Fluminense University where I also dropped out. The years of study at the National School of Statistical Sciences after marrying in 1975, were helpful in my intellectual development, but they didn't give me what I desired most.

That same lack of enthusiasm for studying extended to work. Of course, I remained a competent employee and performed my duties responsibly, but lost interest in the goals that I once thought were so important. I was already made head of treasury at the Rio de Janeiro lottery office and my shift was only four hours a day. At the time, I also worked at the Brazilian Institute of Geography and Statistics, IBGE, organizing the 1970 Census.

But nothing fulfilled me. My dream was to preach the gospel.

My young adulthood was defined by the decision to change direction after my experience with God. I understood that not everyone is chosen to preach the gospel full time, but I wanted to help, to contribute in any way. I wanted to do my share in establishing the Kingdom of God on this earth.

Like everyone who is born again, I was aware that I had been saved to save—through offerings, evangelizing in slums, prisons, and hospitals, and helping with spiritual activities in places where those who are suffering live. But New Life Church did not deem me fit for the service of the work of God, a situation I'll get to later.

That desire was seared into me. I met Ester's mother after we began dating and she viewed me through the same negative lens as the high command of the church, and I immediately sent the message.

"Look, I'm going to preach the gospel in Africa. I am going to go out into this world to save the suffering, whatever it takes," I announced decidedly.

It was an unquenchable thirst. I attended the services at the recently built headquarters of New Life with indignation pulsing through my veins. The old church building was history. The beauty of the new building did nothing for me. I left the services restless, frustrated, and unrecognizable.

The passion for soul winning got to my nerves.

Still I continued to participate actively in the meetings, seeking the Lord Jesus with integrity and sincerity, listening and learning about the Word of God, wanting more and more from the Holy Spirit. However, my irritation would not allow me to rest.

"I don't understand you, Edir," Ester would comment. "We had such a wonderful worship time, such a special seeking of God's presence, and you're so irritated..."

That is what tormented me. Five to six hundred "chosen ones" gathered to worship the Lord, enjoying moments of bliss before the altar, while millions of desperate people, blinded by a false faith, at the church door and outside. And there I was, unable be used in this battle for the lost.

My resentment increased day by day. Another time when I was leaving a worship service at New Life the backed-up traffic made me lose my temper. I had just bought a new VW Beetle with the savings from my salary at the lottery office. When I left the parking lot, all the traffic was at a standstill. A bus was blocking my way. All of a sudden, I turned the steering wheel and rushed to pass it through a narrow space between the bus and a tree on the sidewalk.

Impatient and restless, I gradually accelerated, determined to squeeze through. "You won't make it, Edir," Ester warned me. "I've go to, I will!" I replied. "You won't maaaake it, Edir!" Ester insisted.

The light turned red and my Beetle was trapped between the bus and the tree on the curb. When the light turned green, of course, the bus driver wasn't about to let me pass him. Even so, I shifted into first gear and gunned it. I shot off, leaving behind two floor boards of my new Beetle, one on the tree and the other under the bus. But I made it through, and drove on.

That's how it was. I would leave the services at church all worked up. When I reminisce over the past with Ester, we sort out a lot of things that we didn't understand about each other back then. She remembers that she couldn't figure out why I was so upset all the time.

"The meeting would be so nice and wonderful, but his determination to win souls was stronger," Ester explains. "He seemed like a lion in a cage counting the seconds to freedom."

One Wednesday evening, I had the exact vision of my constant inner conflict. The pastors invited everyone to stand up for the time of worship.

"Let's enter the holy place and present our incense of praise to our God," he said over the microphone. "Come forward, people. All together now, close your eyes."

The church was crowded. The organ played music that drew the believers up to the altar.

I may enter the holy place
and praise your shining face... ...The censer I will sway
and with glory I shall praise.
I shall give to my Lord spiritual offerings[9]

9 *"Posso entrar no santo lugar/ e contemplar seu rosto a brilhar.../ ...O incensário moverei/ E com louvores adorarei./ Ministrarei ao meu Senhor/ ofertas espirituais"*

It was like the congregation of those chosen in heaven. A chorus of angels redeemed before the throne of the Almighty. But even so, a strange feeling took over me. I was flooded with an immense sadness, a boundless agony.

A deafening sound was coming from outside the church. Desperate shouts.

"Have compassion on us! For the love of God, have compassion!"

I had my eyes closed but was fully aware of where I was and what I was thinking. I had a clear image of desperate men and women pleading with cries for help, but being tossed one by one into hell. "What is this frightening scene, my God? All those people thrown into eternal torment as we worship? This is wrong—here we are in the warmth of the church, offering praises and hallelujahs, while people outside are groaning in misery. It's impossible to please God this way. How many people are going to hell, while I'm here just thinking about myself?"

In the hours and days after that meeting, the same questions would be repeated in my mind.

"Why had God given me that vision? What does He want from me? What would He do in my place? After all, what is the highest expression of gratitude to my Lord: praising Him, or saving souls?" I would question myself. "If the Lord Jesus were here, what would He do? What is of more value to God?"

I came to the conclusion that I could not join the worshippers in church, but must seek for the lost.

The Proverbs of King Solomon said it right. "Like one who takes away a garment in cold weather, and like vinegar on soda, is one who sings songs to a heavy heart." (Proverbs 25:20).

I was thirsting to give of myself and be used in body, soul, and spirit as a pastor or in some position doing the work of God. It didn't matter what. I wanted to be an instrument of the Holy Spirit with the single, glorious goal of saving souls.

That conviction was like a fire. A burning, yearning spirit was pulsing within me. It was a calling.

My dreams would be the dreams of God. I was stubbornly determined about taking a radical turn in the direction of my life, but before I did that, I would have to overcome several obstacles.

CHAPTER 3

A SICKNESS THAT BROUGHT LIFE

Sixteen chapters earlier

Faith is action. Perhaps you've heard me speak extensively on this subject. This phrase has almost become a motto of the Universal Church because it so aptly summarizes thoughts of the Bible that I have been preaching about for close to four decades. No matter how much faith we claim to have, there can be no concrete results without action, movement, and taking a stand... No matter how much burning passion I have in me for lost souls, no matter how intense my zeal is to save a crowd of non-believers, I can only be of use to God when I take action.

I was a faithful member of an evangelical church for 11 years, from just before my conversion at 19, up to the mid-1970s. It was 11 years of conformity. Born of God and sealed with the Holy Spirit, but imprisoned in an organization that regarded me as incapable of being used to spread the gospel, I awoke when I decided to take action.

Action changes everything.

Zacchaeus, the tax collector, decided to give away half of all he had to the poor and pay back anyone he had robbed, four times the amount. Before that, he had climbed a tree to catch a glimpse of Jesus coming in to Jericho. Zacchaeus' actions caused the Son of God to choose to visit his house visit, over all the other people present. And salvation came to that house. At a house full of people in Capernaum, the Lord Jesus saw a paralytic being lowered from the rooftop by four of his friends, and a miracle happened. Staring certain death in the face at the hand of Pharaoh's armies, Moses heard a rebuke from God: "Why are you crying out to me? Tell the Israelites to move on." (Exodus 14:15)

God was waiting for his action. I needed to move.

At New Life Church they did not believe I had the "anointing" even to open and close the doors at service times. I waited for a prolonged period of time, an eternity for me, for a chance. Eleven years later, I was convinced I could wait no longer. It was time for a turnaround.

One Wednesday evening I asked to speak to one of the main leaders of the church, Bishop Tito Oscar. A few days earlier I had begged my brother-in-law Pastor Jorcelino Queiroz, who was married to one of Ester's sisters, for an opportunity to help. He was, at the time, in charge of a small church in Teresópolis, on a mountain range in Rio de Janeiro. The church had no more than 20 people attending, and I was prepared to contribute to its growth.

I anxiously drove up the almost 90 kilometers of mountain road. Since I was a little uneasy when I approached Jorcelino, I got straight to the point:

"Pastor, I want to help you. Let's reach out to this whole town together and fill this church. I'm sure it'll work. It can't be that difficult!"

Jorcelino wasn't sure of my motives. He took a deep breath and replied.

"There's nothing I can do, Edir. You know... I'm under Bishop Tito. Everything I do has to be authorized by him."

"Okay, then I'll speak to him, Pastor. I'll ask to be allowed to help you," I happily replied. "I believe we'll win so many souls in this city!"

"If he authorizes it, fine. His word is final," he said, ending the conversation.

On my way back to Rio, my eyes were shining. I saw a real opportunity to help spread the gospel. On the drive home, the dappled hues of green on the trees of the Atlantic Forest, and views of the mountain peaks from the highway seemed to open a curtain to an ideal world. Could this be the beginning of everything? Would the Holy Spirit make use of me from this moment on? Would God touch the hearts of the leadership of New Life Church? Would the pastors believe in my potential and desire to serve on the altar? Will someone notice me at last?

That Wednesday evening I was ready to talk to Bishop Tito. Our talk took place in the meeting room of the church.

"Bishop, I talked to Pastor Jorcelino and there are things I could do to help his work in Teresópolis. The church is small and there's so much room for growth! I'm sure, Bishop Tito, that there are lots of ways the work could grow," I pleaded, with a hopeful face.

He just looked at me and gave a slight nod.

"All I need is one opportunity. I've attended church here for many years and I want to save souls. I need to save souls! I feel that God's asking me to do it! I have to do something!" I said, revealing what was going on inside. "My only desire, Bishop, is to obey what the Lord Jesus commands: 'Go into all the world and preach the Gospel to every creature.'"

Tito Oscar got up from his chair and with a tone of authority typical of traditional religious pontificating, set off to shatter my dream.

"Edir, young man, pay attention. Never forget what I'm about to say. Before Christ stated, 'Go into all the world and preach the Gospel to every creature,' He said many other things. That verse is in the last chapter of Mark, but to get there, you have to start with the first chapter. Do you understand, Edir?"

I did not want to give up so I opened up and told him what I felt inside.

"Bishop Tito, I have been born of God and baptized in the Holy Spirit... What else do I need? Please, allow me to save souls!"

"Edir, you know that's not the way we work. We are a cell group church," he replied.

The cell group system was adopted by the New Life Church in the 1960s, from the movement of a then famous Argentinean pastor Juan Carlos Ortiz. He founded the largest Pentecostal Church in Buenos Aires at the time and spread his shepherding/discipleship movement throughout Latin America, including Brazil. Cell groups consisted of

Bible classes for small groups of neighbors and acquaintances at the home of a church member. Cell leaders were sent two by two and were hand-picked by the ministry leaders.

I questioned the limitations of the concept.

"What about the Indians, Bishop? How will they be reached if we limit ourselves to this type of outreach? Ideally, we should continue this outreach but apply other types of outreach tpp. If we continue down this path, how will we ever reach Indian tribes?"

"Edir, that is not exactly how it is..." he began, but I had had it. I admit, I lost my patience.

"Well, this is how it is, Bishop. I want to let you know that I'm leaving your church."

He was stunned. I went on.

"I don't know whether Ester will join me. But whether she goes with me or not, I'm leaving. The decision is made."

The conversation ended there. I stormed out of the church. Ester says this was my first major revolt. I was married, had one daughter, Cristiane, who had been dedicated on New Life Church's altar two years before. But at that moment, I was not worried about my family or anything else.

It was a moment of decision.

Jacob wrestled with God until he got what he wanted. Fearlessly, he demonstrated that it is impossible to transform a problem by conforming to it. A spirit of war is needed to grab hold of God's promises. Jacob wrestled with God until daybreak. "And He said, 'Let Me go, for the day breaks.' But he said, 'I will not let You go unless You bless me!' So He said to him, 'What is your name?' He said, 'Jacob.' And He said, 'Your name shall no longer be called Jacob, but Israel; for you have struggled with God and with men, and have prevailed.'" (Genesis 32:26-28)

From that day on, I intensified my zeal for anything that involved spreading the Word of God, until the Holy Spirit revealed a clear path for me to follow—that is, until I was given an opportunity to preach the gospel on the altar. I had done this on my own for a number of years. Since the church had not wanted to make use of me, I went out and talked about faith in various pockets of misery and suffering in Rio de Janeiro, while still working at the lottery office and keeping up with my own life.

A cloud that won't leave

When I was single, the person who joined me on those outings was my current brother-in-law, Romildo Ribeiro Soares, married to my youngest sister, Magdalena. We had all met in New Life Church's youth group. I met Soares for the first time in 1968 and after that we began to go out to share our faith with others every now and then.

I used to ride with him to places where we did volunteer work, including the Oscar Clark Hospital in the Maracanã district, right next to the stadium (one of the largest in the world). It was a rehabilitation clinic for people with fractures and permanent or temporary physical disabilities. I saw very touching scenes of men, women, and even children struggling to recover the use of their legs and arms. We entered that environment to bring a message of support and trust to the sick and their next of kin.

I would walk up to the beds, one by one, and lead patients to a small room the hospital had reserved for prayer. Many arrived on stretchers, legs in casts or suspended in the air to make sure fluid would not accumulate. Others came in with bandaged hands or arms in slings. The most serious cases, paralysis of the lower body and serious spinal cord injuries, would be accompanied by a nurse. Every Saturday morning or afternoon we made this sacrifice with a single goal: save souls for the Kingdom of Heaven.

Since Soares was shy, I always gave a word of faith followed by a prayer. He would organize the showing of a film clip on miracles. He admired North American evangelist T.L. Osborn, known for his books, films, and documentaries about mass healings, which he periodically received from the evangelist himself, showing rallies in Europe, Africa, and elsewhere in the world. Osborn even sent a small film projector to Soares to help him with his outreach.

We decided to broaden our outreach to the poor and neglected areas of Rio de Janeiro. And so we began the same type of work in various underprivileged areas, and in particular, Rocinha (literal translation, little farm), already one of the largest slums or "favelas" in Brazil. We always did the same thing. We would spend four or five days distributing hundreds of leaflets in the alleyways of the slum, inviting residents to an Osborn film. Then on the appointed day after the presentation, I would pray for broken families, the sick, unemployed, addicts, prostitutes, and other people living on the margins of society.

When Bishop Robert McAlister, founder of New Life Church, heard that I had left the church, he asked me to come in for a private conversation, along with Ester. He was polite and respectful, and let us know that he was unhappy with the news and asked me not to take any drastic actions.

"Bishop Robert, as I explained to Bishop Tito, for years I've been waiting for an opportunity that never comes. I can't bear for our church to enjoy the presence of God in comfort while people are suffering outside. I want to save souls, but I'm not allowed to!"

He listened patiently, said he understood, and then asked to talk to Ester in private.

"Relax. This is nothing but flash in the pan, Ester. Don't worry. Edir is over excited. I really want both of you to stay in our church," McAlister said.

Ester was silent. She merely bowed her head. She knew what was going on inside of me.

"Keep calm, Ester. I assure you, what Edir is experiencing is no more than a passing cloud."

Ester attended New Life Church for three more months, attending Wednesday and Sunday services, waiting for the cloud to pass. But the "weather forecast" was different—this cloud would never pass. I left New Life Church, and thank God the sun continually shined for me.

After leaving New Life on my own, I continued with my evangelistic outreaches. I had already taken on a new direction in life. I was confident of what I wanted. I was determined not to turn back. But what exactly would I do now? Where should I go? I was not going to transfer to another church. If that was going to be the case, I might as well have stayed with New Life. My dream was to start a church from nothing. But how could I start without support or finances? All I had was the will to do it. My faith pointed in one single direction: I would have to wait.

Although I was disappointed at being judged incapable, I left New Life Church with no resentment or regret toward anyone. Quite the opposite. That is where I had learned about the gospel, tithing, and good character. That is where I met Ester, where we got married, and where we had dedicated our daughter to God.

When I left I never once bad-mouthed the church, and made it known to anyone that asked, that it was the place where I had my encounter with God and was baptized in the Holy Spirit. At the time I maintained a friendly relationship with the bishops and pastors of the congregation and never dared to convince friends or acquaintances to leave. It would have been neither fair, nor loyal. The strongest proof of this is that my wife and daughter remained there after I left.

Currently, many pastors leave the Universal Church with hateful and vengeful attitudes. They take their hands off of the plow and then turn around and sow seeds of anger, cynicism, cowardice, and take derogatory potshots. They don't show the least bit of respect or gratitude to me or the other bishops, pastors, and assistants who helped them when they first walked in, oppressed by demons. But worst of all, they show no gratitude to God.

Curiously, this behavior is a carbon copy of how evil spirits act when they are cast out of the people they have enslaved. Filled with rage, they swear and scream that they hate me, hate the Universal Church, and hate others who are doing the work of God. Why do so many pastors and bishops leave the church and feel gratified to spread so much resentment? Why do they take pleasure in angrily criticizing those who reached into the gutter to help them when they needed it most? The "gospel of hate" is beyond comprehension, tragic, and demonic, and is practiced only by those who do not belong to God. That is the harsh, undiluted truth. But they are human beings who need our forgiveness and continued prayers.

Alone and disconnected from New Life Church, I continued my work with Romildo Soares. Like me, he wanted to spend his life involved with the things of faith. That was when he brought up another Pentecostal church that he wanted join and work with as a pastor. It was called House of Blessing, and at that time was being led by Pastor Cecílio Carvalho Fernandes.

For the very first time I saw demons manifesting and people boldly casting them out. I went to watch the deliverance meetings very few times, but often enough to completely remove any fear of facing the devil. I saw evil confronted in an unflinching way, but I missed the teachings of the Word of God that were so present and meaningful in New Life Church. Step by step the Spirit of God led me to imagine the ideal model for a church. A work capable of shaking the foundations of hell. A formula began to form in my heart and mind. An inspiration from above.

Before I did anything about this, Soares left New Life for the House of Blessing with another church member and colleague, Samuel Coutinho. At Soares' insistence, I decided to join them, with the hope that I would be noticed when it came time to raise up pastors. After a short while, both were consecrated as pastors by Cecílio Carvalho. But not me. Cecílio promised to raise me up, but said that I should wait for a lengthy period of time to gain experience.

"Edir, you are not yet ready. I'm going to need to see you develop, only then can I raise you as a pastor," Cecílio affirmed.

Another "no" in my life. Once again, no one could see any strength or talent in me. I was brushed aside one more time, excluded, belittled. While kneeling in prayer in my room, all by myself, I repeatedly asked for the reason for so much frustration.

"Why doesn't anyone notice me, Lord? Do they just want to kill my excitement? All I want to do is serve You with all of my life," I would say to God.

It seemed like there was a huge conspiracy to force me to give up.

In the thick of that spiritual struggle, one event pushed me to an all-or-nothing stance. Another moment of conviction that would transform my life.

PUNCHES

"Ma'am, where's my daughter? Where's my daughter? I want to see my daughter!"

This was my plea to the nurses at the Rio de Janeiro Servants Assistance Institute maternity house on the morning of Sunday, January 20, 1975. The medical team's attitude was frustrating. Why had this mother still not seen her baby three days after she had been born? I imagined that something was wrong. As soon as our child had been born, she was taken to have her foot reflexes tested and had not returned.

Ester was still under the effect of the anesthesia from the caesarean section when her child had been born that Friday, and wasn't sure what had happened when they took her away. I was not allowed to be present during the birth, the common procedure of public hospitals in those days. Fathers were only permitted in to see the mothers on visiting days, like that dark Sunday morning.

When the effects of the anesthesia had worn off, Ester repeatedly asked about our daughter, but it was in vain. She would see other women being handed their babies to nurse, but received no news of our baby. As a precaution, news of anything out of the ordinary could only be explained when the child's father was present, since nobody knew how the mother would react. I walked into the room, impatient.

"Where's our daughter, Ester?"

"I don't know, Edir. The nurse won't tell me anything. She keeps saying they're giving her a bath, but won't show me our baby," Ester replied, still in bed. "I'm worried. See if you can find out something."

I set off down the hospital corridor, asking about our child. Suddenly, the head nurse called me into a corner and asked me to wait while she looked up our child's name.

"Yes, it's Viviane. Viviane Rangel Bezerra," I confirmed.

"Please relax, sir. She'll be here soon. Stay calm," she said, slightly shaken. Then she asked me to follow her into a room.

I waited anxiously. A few minutes later, two physicians came up to me and attempted to prepare me for a sight that would affect me forever. The nurse handed me our baby, whose appearance was impossible to forget. She was extremely thin, had dark circles under her eyes and her face was deformed. There was a gaping wound on the gums of her mouth, part of her upper lip was missing, and there was a hole where the roof of her mouth should have been.

"This is a birth defect, but other than this she's healthy," the physician explained in an attempt to comfort me. "It's called a cleft palate, a congenital malformation."

"Well, I don't want that!" I reacted angrily, before I could think about what I was saying.

When we went into the room Ester anxiously locked her eyes on me.

"It's not a pretty sight, my love, you have to be strong," I said to her, grabbing one of her hands.

When I looked at Ester again, I could not contain myself. She was attempting to wipe away her tears, but her face was soaked. I also cried. Both of us wept for a few minutes in silence. Then something exploded inside of me that lifted my mind up to God. My body was possessed with an unfathomable strength. My pain transported me directly to the throne of God. I felt the pain of the rejection my daughter would have to go through at school, in her childhood and adolescence, perhaps even for the rest of her life. My thoughts wandered to her first years of school and projected into her future. I lived the past and the future in that instant. True torment.

However, instead of seeking comfort in my family or the church, I confronted the problem head on with uncontrollable rage. I decided to pray. But it was not a normal prayer. I clenched my fists in anger and threw punches at the bed countless times.

"God, no one is going to stop me now. Not my family, not my wife, not the future, not feelings, nothing. No one can stop me now! No one! No one! I've had enough!"

That was the birth of the Universal Church of the Kingdom of God.

My revolt was not against God, but against hell, which was causing the pain that I felt at that very moment in the lives of millions of human beings around the world. Once and for all, I was determined to place 100 percent of my life on the altar. I decided to surrender myself like I had never done before, even if no church or pastor believed in my ability to serve God. I would pay any price to help the suffering and rejected. I left the hospital mid-afternoon and went to my mother's apartment in the southern part of Rio. So at Mrs. Geninha's my family learned about Viviane's problem. Obviously, I was very sad, but at the same time confident of my actions from that moment on.

"I will not be angry at God; I'm angry at the devil. Now I'm going to invade hell and rescue those who are lost," I said to my brothers, nephews, and cousins.

When I went home I meditated on that terrible Sunday. Whatever thought came to my mind, one goal flooded my being: more than ever, I was determined to leave my job, give up my personal plans and help those who were suffering and far from God. Time was of the essence. I'd been hit hard with the reality of what suffering really was.

It was impossible not to think about the hardships Viviane would have to face throughout her life. I had grown up with a physical disability. I knew what it was like. The memory of Viviane's wretched state made me recall my own birth defect. I looked at my hands. The congenital defect left my fingers slightly bent, flawed. That had caused an inferiority complex throughout my childhood. I imagined how difficult it would be for an teenage girl to overcome a facial defect, the part of a woman's appearance that's most important to her.

I also thought about the financial hardships that would arise with Viviane's disability. Everything was telling me not to leave my job to preach the Word of God. Our budget was already stretched, and the two pregnancies that brought our daughters into the world had not been planned. Seven months after Cristiane was born, we were surprised with another pregnancy. The news had even frightened us.

Ester and I had used the pill and condoms, but in the end they had not worked for us. When Viviane arrived I had no other choice. I started working more to increase our income, but even that was not enough. I relied on help from my brother Celso who was a flight attendant at the time. He would kindly bring over meat and other groceries every once in a while.

Ester stayed in the hospital for another five days. When she came home, we started the long struggle of keeping Viviane healthy and strong. It was not easy. Feeding her was a daily challenge. She could not be breastfed because she could not create suction with her mouth. Even using a spoon to dribble milk drop by drop into her mouth could easily lead to choking because she had no roof to her mouth. Ten days after she arrived home Viviane began to choke as she was being fed and started to turn blue.

Ester was screaming.

"Edir, O my God! She's not breathing. Do something... do something... she's going to die!"

I did not know what to do. Viviane was not breathing. There was no time to pray. I raised her as high as I could and shouted:

"Jesus!"

Vivian coughed and started breathing again. That was proof of my unlimited love for her.

MOTHER OF WAR

As Viviane grew, new complications arose. She was sickly, caught persistent colds easily and urinary tract infections. When she was a year old, she underwent her first surgery. The procedure was painful for us and for her. In total, she went through twelve surgeries before she became a teenager. Before each one, as any child would be, she would get very anxious. We didn't know what to do to calm her down. After each operation, she would throw up a lot of blood because of the major surgical procedures being performed on her face.

There was so much bitterness, so much suffering. Up until today I cannot think about those events without wanting to cry.

It was a very difficult phase in our lives, which in turn, brought about the salvation of millions of souls all over the world. The Universal Church was given birth that January of 1975. I had no doubt about which path to follow. Even as a faithful member struggling for opportunities in a church, my only desire was to save souls. I was upset about not being given the opportunity to preach the gospel, despite my continual insistence.

Viviane's birth triggered my shout for independence. If she had not been born sick, the Universal Church would not exist today. My revolt would still be lying dormant, and I might have gone back to being a simple member of New Life Church. But my suffering meant that I could preach about suffering. The Universal Church does not preach about things that can be learned in schools or universities, but rather practical lessons of life from the Holy Spirit.

Amazingly, and as unimaginable as it may seem for any mother of a sick child, Viviane's pain was good for Ester. That's right. It caused Ester to be refined as a woman of God. She was my heroine, especially during Viviane's childhood and adolescent years. Her importance to me became increasingly clear during that distressing period of our life.

It was up to Ester to handle the childhood crises that came as a result of Viviane's disability, in silence and without complaining. She was bullied at school, especially when we lived in the United States. Her classmates would make fun of her because of her mouth.

Though she was being given speech therapy, Viviane had trouble speaking, which made it difficult for her to be understood and was annoying to her. The only person who easily understood her was Cristiane. The older sister became the younger sister's protector. They became confidantes and were inseparable. Psychiatrists told us that Viviane's trauma would never be erased, even in adulthood, but her encounter with the Lord Jesus eliminated those negative feelings, just as had happened to me.

Ester had been so happy with the arrival of our first daughter. She constantly heard compliments about the beauty and sweetness of little Cristiane. She loved taking photos to chronicle her first years of life. But when Viviane arrived, Ester faced the complete opposite reaction. When she took the bus to the hospital for Viviane's treatments, people who saw a glimpse of her gasped and stepped back in shock.

"Many women would say that it was bad luck," Ester recalls, and because of these insensitive reactions of people, she would frequently return home feeling very low. "I saw women smoking with perfectly healthy babies on their laps, and here was my daughter in this situation. I'd wonder, why me, when I've tried to live a wholesome life before God?"

As we went over the past in preparation for this book, Ester revealed something I had never known about.

"Before we got married my mother warned me: 'Are you sure you want to marry him? Your children might have the same disability he has,'" she recalled. "I always replied: 'God won't allow that.' She was worried about me. But we both know now that Viviane's disability was not related to Edir in any way."

God allowed that to happen for a reason. He has never made anything defective. Those two things don't go together. How could a perfect being create something imperfect? Impossible. But even beyond that, I do not believe, my mind does not allow me to believe, that God is responsible for the conception of children. Human beings conceive children. God gave His creatures the ability to conceive, but He does not interfere in this fixed law of life.

Even some of our relatives were shocked with our child's appearance and when I saw Ester being subjected to that, I suffered alone, in silence. I carried that sense wherever I went. At the same time, this pain united us. We wept together. We also overcame together. We strengthened our connection. We grew. What's more, Ester became even more sensitive to the suffering of those who were living far from a life of faith. In the future, we would combine forces in a tireless journey to rescue the suffering.

A long time has passed. Viviane is now a perfect 37-year-old married woman. In a letter of celebration to Ester she explained in further detail what only she had experienced during that bitter time, detailing many situations we could never have imagined, and made a touching disclosure.

Dear Mother,

Who in life has had the strength to love me? Who believed in me, even in moments when no one else would?

Though my appearance was shocking, she found the strength to fight, to believe that there was a way out even though all the experts insisted that my problem would never be fixed, and would only worsen as I grew, causing trauma and insecurity.

What a cruel pain for someone to swallow, what a hardship in her path. She confronted the very first hurdles of my physical disability. She heard everyone's criticisms. She dealt with the problem up close, and then made sure she was strong for the rest of her family.

During surgeries, when I was filled with fear, she comforted me. Only she could do that. Her presence assured me. Her care brought me a sense of protection. Her affection made me confident that everything would be all right.

Who taught me the moral principles that I abide by to this very day? And why did her words bring so much strength to my being? Because she was, and is, balanced. Nothing could make her lose control, even when I arrived home after surgery and was angry.

She knew how to control things. She soothed me with her wise manner of instruction. She would teach my older sister to give up certain things for me.

As a five-year-old girl it was hard to discover my physical shortcomings and that my speech was not the same as other children's. What a moment! All hell broke loose. I came face to face with contempt and prejudice from people outside my family.

And what happened?

My loving mother fulfilled her duty flawlessly. She was not aware of the problems I faced at school, and that I felt like an alien whenever we left to go somewhere. She was always the attentive, caring mother who covered me with kisses. She made me forget all the turmoil I felt outside. I was safe at home.

I was kept safe and was educated. She used her authority to set limits, but did not stop there. She taught morals as well. She continually helped me to see that I needed to change, not others. She taught us to value others, to appreciate work, to serve, to honor, and to love without limits!

Above all of this, she taught me to be careful of my own instincts. In fact, she was an essential part of my acknowledgement of God.

She helped me to see harsh realities. The truth was painful, and I often struggled with the truth, but there was no other path to take—the principles were already there, and those principles were fear and respect.

My dear mother, I want you to know that to this very day I strive to show you how grateful I am for everything you were and did for me. You will never die inside of me! Never! No matter how much my life changes, your advice will remain under lock and key. And you know what, Mother? Every single piece of your advice did me good.

I love you, and will shout it from the rooftops for everyone to hear the love and appreciation that I have for you. I can only give daughters one piece of advice: honor your father and mother, since we owe our lives to their sacrifices.

Viviane de Freitas

A short time ago, Cristiane, my oldest daughter also wrote down some experiences she went through with her sister in the struggle with her physical disability. Siblings often have special relationships, even indescribable bonds. These words translate her unique impressions and are proof of the impact that Viviane's illness had on our family.

My sister was my best friend and I was hers. Unfortunately, one of us was always in the shadow of the other, and though it could not have been different, a small part of us was deeply affected by that.

Her birth defect made her crave attention, and to relieve her pain, our family and friends paid more attention to her. The fact that I did not have a birth defect made me feel terrible guilt, and led me to settle into always being in her shadow.

Vivi grew up accustomed to attention, and when she did not get it, that would be a problem. I grew up accustomed to the shadows, hiding as much as I could behind people I thought were more deserving.

Although I was eventually baptized with the Holy Spirit as an teenager, I continued to be insecure. Wherever I went, there it was. Whatever I did, it was there to bother me. With every person I met, it rose to the surface in a terrible way.

So I became known as the "boring" sister, "the one likely to marry late in life," and most of all, whenever people called me, they would mistakenly call me by my sister's name... "Oh, that's right, you're the other one, Cristiane, right?" That would usually be followed by: "I always confuse your names." But that never happened to my sister... interesting.

Instead of getting offended with these comments or reacting to them, I would always interpret them as proof of the already distorted image I had of myself. That's right, I'm not as funny as my sister. Yes, my conversations are boring. Yes, I am shy. I will have a very hard time finding someone to love me as I am. That's right, I am not as brave as my sister, nor as strong. I thought, maybe it's better to remain here in the shadow of everyone else in my life.

My marriage changed all that, though not immediately. It took me years to rid myself of all the baggage I had been carrying since childhood. But when I finally did, my marriage changed completely. I felt attractive for the first time in my life. I let my hair grow long, and it has been so ever since. It's strange how our looks are linked to the way we feel inside.

"What was the secret?" you may ask.

Faith. I started to believe in myself without having to see anything. I would do what God placed in my heart, without worrying about how incapable or small I was, and then He started to make use of me. I began to understand that the less capable we are the more He makes use of us, so I made the most of it!

Cristiane Cardoso

Like Cristiane, Viviane is now married to a man of God. She is a fulfilled, happy woman with many dreams, and most importantly, she has dedicated her life to the gospel like me. Her disability has been left behind. It is part of a dark past that is only remembered to understand the meaning of everything that happened.

But the most valuable thing to arise from that period was the explosion of indignation that I had felt since the first years of encountering God. The Universal Church was given birth at that moment, when through faith and courage to approach God with revolt and boldness.

Viviane's birth woke me up once and for all.

Faith moves me, it affects my inner being. It is pure, it is free of emotion, and is given birth when I stop to think. I think about a promise from God and look at my life. Why has this not yet come true? I am supposed to have a happy life according to the words of Jesus, so why is it completely ruined? Why am I bitter and living in agony?

Faith makes my blood boil. It has an impact on my mind, invades my intelligence, and makes me restless, even irritated. God does not change. God wants to appear to me and to everyone else who believes. This happened with the heroes in the Bible. David threw down the gauntlet with the giant. Elijah challenged the prophets of Baal. Joshua knocked down the walls of a city. Moses faced down Pharaoh's armies. Gideon dared to ask where the God of his parents was, who had done wonders in the past, but had not appeared in his life. These are not mythological fairytales nor imaginations of a man's mind. They are real.

Faith was pushing me. It was time to make a move on my destiny.

I PAVED THE WAY

A few months after Viviane's dramatic birth, I was already an evangelical preacher, but did not have my own ministry. The former members of New Life Church, Romildo Soares and Samuel Coutinho, invited me for the grand opening the Eternal Path Crusade. Coutinho was president, Soares was vice president, and I was treasurer, a function I already performed professionally at the lottery. Although I held that position, I never performed any financial duties in the administration of the new Church, which officially opened in 1975.

The evangelistic work was different. The Crusade was a single entity, but each person ran their own ministry separately. Because of my lack of experience and because I was simply an evangelist, most of the time I ended up assisting my brother-in-law with his preaching in the northern zone of Rio de Janeiro, although sometimes I would help spread Coutinho's work as well. He established his church in the district of Jacarepaguá in the western zone.

In the little free time I had, I talked about the Lord Jesus in both the rich districts and poor regions of the city. There were some areas where I wouldn't dare bring Ester along. The Gardênia Azul community in lower Jacarepaguá, for example, was a constant focus of our outreach. The slums—or stilt houses—were part of a sad, cruel aspect of our unjust society.

I handed out flyers, helped the sick, and gathered the unemployed, the elderly, women, and children for prayers in the community center. I would tread the wooden walkways, which were one-and-a-half meters above the ground and permeated with the filth of sewage and industrial waste, to invite the residents to learn about the Crusade. The place was a stage for endless shoot-outs between the police and drug traffickers, or between criminal gangs fighting over their turf. Yet people respected me all the time. Many would even ask for prayer for protection from the gang wars or to be freed from the underworld of crime. Samuel Coutinho was the only one who would join me.

In the Cidade de Deus—City of God—we put forth the same effort to serve the outcasts. It had been in existence for fewer than 20 years and was built according to policies to remove the shanty towns— "favelas"—from other areas of Rio de Janeiro. The name, City of God, had an impressive, attractive sound for new residents. But that "city" had nothing to do with God. Its inhabitants could only hope for a better life.

I continued to work hard. I was a dedicated evangelist on breaks during the week and served full time on weekends. I had to support my household. In addition to my job at the lottery, I started doing extra work teaching private math classes. Ester still stayed on with New Life Church, but she would join me for certain meetings.

In the northern zone, Romildo Soares' ministry was not growing, and I would take those opportunities to gain more experience and win souls. I performed several services, even without knowing how to preach or how to carry out deliverance. Soares had a habit of canceling the gatherings due to few attendants.

At the time, we would rent out a movie theater for a few hours during a series of weekdays to perform special meetings, the so-called "Campaigns of Faith." The rent was not cheap. Once the lease was confirmed, we would go out on the streets to invite people to the services. If the meetings brought enough people, the work would continue. Otherwise, we would look for another movie theater in a different region of the city.

This happened in what was formerly an adult movie theater, São José, in Tiradentes Square in downtown Rio de Janeiro. The stakes were high: Soares decided to pay for the first publicity campaign on the radio to fill the service with people. He spent what was about five thousand reais[10] at the time of his own money, a small fortune for someone who was not financially stable at the time. He ordered hundreds of flyers, which I handed out around practically all the streets in the area. I went from door to door, giving the invitation. On the appointed day, we were really disappointed. The event didn't bring in any more than 40 people. When I walked up

10 About $2500 today.

to the pulpit, I could see the misery in my brother-in-law's expression. After that, I always led the meetings with that small number of believers.

At the Méier Cinema the scene repeated itself. The first meeting brought in less than 100 people, and Soares was discouraged once again. I was put in charge of all meetings that brought 20 to 30 people for a long time. In the city of Rio Bonito, located in the countryside near Niterói, we went through the same thing. It was difficult driving three hours for Saturday meetings when only twenty believers at most would show up.

In all those places, I always did my best. In the Bruni Piedade Cinema, for example, the meetings were almost empty; but in my mind, I had the image of a church crowded with millions of people. I would pray, sing, and transmit faith with all my strength. Those who saw me preaching couldn't believe I'd put in so much effort for such a small group of people. I didn't care. I wanted to do my best for my God. I wanted to save people for Jesus. I would see the invisible because I always believed in the meaning of faith. "Now faith is the substance of things hoped for, the evidence of things not seen." (Hebrews 11:1).

The meetings that brought larger groups of people were always led by Soares and Samuel Coutinho, and I'd try to assist as much as I could. As usual, I would hand out flyers before the gatherings, rain or shine.

A few minutes before each meeting, we'd always perform the same ritual. It could not be altered. I would greet the public over the microphone and with grandiose words, over sensational background music, announce who was about to come to the altar.

"Good evening, people of God! Shortly, we shall be receiving the prayer from the great man of God, Missionary R.R. Soares! Wait and see!"

Three musicians sang and played along with a female believer of the Crusade. The choruses were interrupted when I started to announce the "great missionaries."

"In a few moments, the prayer of faith and manifestation of power from one of the most respected ministers of the Gospel in Rio de Janeiro: Missionary Samuel Coutinho! Wait and see!"

I would then prompt the people to applaud. Only one or two would respond.

In hindsight, it's impossible not to learn lessons from those moments I experienced as an evangelist. Without a doubt, they were some of the most reprehensible customs in the evangelical world. I obeyed because I was a servant, a mere coworker, but I never saw it in a positive light. After all, they were ordained pastors and I did not consider it my right to question anointed men.

Vanity among preachers, especially the most traditional ones, goes unchecked and often out of control. King David's prayer says it all: "Yours, Lord, is the greatest and the power and the glory and the majesty and the splendor, for everything in heaven and earth is yours. Yours, Lord, is the kingdom; you are exalted as head over all" (1 Chronicles 29:11). And David said more: "Wealth and honor come from you; you are the ruler of all things. In your hands are strength and power to exalt and give strength to all" (1 Chronicles 29:12).

No further comment.

Graduating from a theology course at the Evangelical Church where I took my first steps in the Christian faith.

The time I started as an evangelist in the north zone of Rio de Janeiro.

The Jardim do Méier pavilion, where I started preaching outdoors, which resulted in loyal members up to the present.

The old funeral parlor building in the Abolição district in Rio de Janeiro, one of the first meetings in the history of the Universal Church of the Kingdom of God. Millions of peo would be rescued following that simple evangelistic work.

On my birthday, Ester knelt beside me as I was consecrated as a pastor in the old funeral parlor, the first church of the Universal Church of the Kingdom of God.

Photos after the consecration ceremony with the wife and daughters of Seu Albino Silva da Costa.

Ester's parents and our family. This is the first time some of these photos of unforgettable moments have been made public.

June 7th, 1980, when I performed the wedding of Bishop Paulo Roberto Guimarães and his wife Solange. At the end of the ceremony, we rushed off to the decisive election that defined the future of the Universal Church.

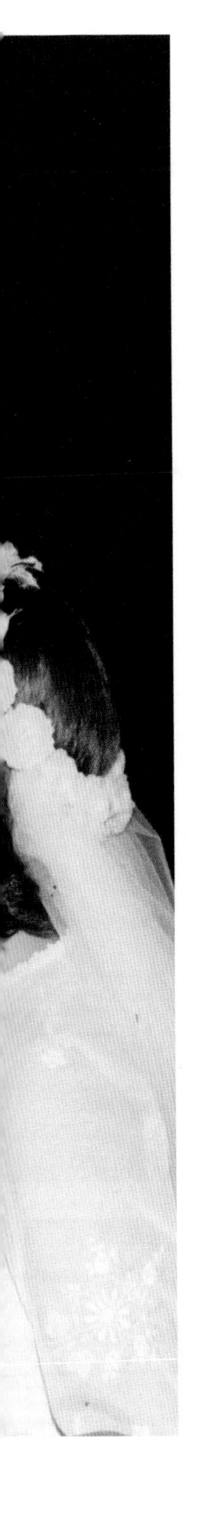

Embracing the first voluntary assistants of the Church, who were later consecrated bishops. On the right, with Renato Maduro, who passed away on December 12th, 2010. Below, with former bishop and former federal congressman, Carlos Rodrigues

Este Cartão, identifica o portador como
MEMBRO desta Igreja, inscrito sob o
N.º 002 na Congregação de ABOLIÇÃO
A Igreja Universal do Reino de Deus solicita as autoridades civis, militares e eclesiásticas se dignem dispensar ao portador todas as facilidades e auxílio no desempenho de sua santa função cristã.

IGREJA UNIVERSAL DO REINO DE DEUS
A IGREJA DA BÊNÇÃO
Sede: - Av. Suburbana, 7.258 - Abolição - RJ.
Insc. 48.382 - Liv. A 8 C.G.C. 29.744.778/0001-97

Nome: ALBINO DA SILVA
Rua: Av. Suburbana N.º 7178/201
Cidade RIO DE JANEIRO Estado RJ.

Assinatura do Portador

Assinatura do Pastor

Seu Albino, the man who found the building of the former funeral parlor, while visiting the construction work for the Temple of Solomon in São Paulo. Also, his card depicting him as member number 2 of the Universal Church.

RIO DE JANEIRO
A recent service I ministered at our Del Castilho branch with thousands of followers
Our faith and objectives are still the same as they were at the time of our foundation

Thirty five years after its birth, the Universal Church of the Kingdom of God has spread all over the world to more than 200 countries. Even greater than its reach, is the number of people who have been rescued from lives of bitterness and misery.

TEXAS
United States

TOKYO
Japan

MANILA
Philippines

BUCHAREST
Romania

LISBON
Portugal

HONG KONG
China

MOZAMBIQUE
Inauguration service I performed at our branch in the capital of Maputo, on March 12th, 2011. A crowd had to watch the gathering outside the church

SOUTH AFRICA
Large meeting of faith in Johannesburg, on Good Friday in 2012. The Ellis Park Stadium, where Brazil played in the World Cup, was too small for the people of the Universal Church.

The day of prayer for the humble in February 2010. Down on our knees, we rip our heart before God. "You will be hated by everyone because of me, but the one who stands firm to the end will be saved" (Matthew 10.22).

THE LORD'S APPROVAL

The most successful Eternal Path Crusade church was actually Samuel Coutinho's in Jacarepaguá. He was known for selling pasta and cookies out of his VW van. Every month or two, I brought some elderly ladies from the Méier Cinema in my Beetle—the few followers from the services that had been given me—to be baptized in Jacarepaguá. The busiest day would gather a maximum of six elderly ladies, while Coutinho's church would be packed with more than 800 people.

Every Friday evening, without exception, there would be a meeting with pastors and their wives and some of the older evangelists at the church president's home. During one of those meetings, around 10 p.m., after greeting everyone, Ester and I found a corner in the room to listen to Samuel Coutinho's pastoral guidance. We arrived anxious for the message of faith because, despite the limitations of our spiritual work, we were motivated in the struggle for lost lives.

Strangely enough, the meeting had only just started, and Coutinho was very harsh with me. He stared me in the eyes and was straightforward:

"Listen, Edir, let me tell you something. Young man, I don't think you have what it takes to do the work of God!"

An embarrassing silence fell over the room.

"I think you really should keep your job at the lottery, earning your daily bread. You don't have what it takes, young man!" he rudely continued.

Other pastors, workers, assistants, and I had shared the same enthusiasm to live out our dream, to quit our jobs to dedicate ourselves 100 percent to the work of God.

"The thing is, I am taking the Bruni Piedade Cinema from you and bringing in my own people. We'll have music and strong prayers, and will fill it up with crowds," he determined harshly. "Do you understand, Edir? It's no good. You really don't have what it takes," he repeated.

"All right, pastor. But I know what I have inside of me," I replied.

"All you have are old ladies, Edir," he said, laughing out loud with scorn.

Those words sounded like a bomb blowing up inside of me. In front of everyone, my passion for souls had been assaulted. My pain was not because I was losing the special work I had been doing, but because once again, I was deemed incapable of winning souls.

That hurt me deeply.

But the Holy Spirit touched me strongly that day.

There were flashes going through my mind like a movie. The same questions came back. When will someone believe in my talent and will? And now, just a few steps away from my dream, will I lose it all again? My encounter with God. The baptism with Breath of Heaven. The 16th chapter of Mark.

The fire of burning straw. The passing cloud. The "no" from the House of Blessing. Viviane, the baby in my arms. The angry punches. The call from the Holy Spirit—none of that could be a lie. What about my revolt of faith? And the real fire that burns in my spirit? My passion for souls?

"My God, I only want to serve you. One opportunity. One chance," I thought. "One yes. Who will say yes to me once?"

Along my path, I had only heard "yes" from my dear mother and my faithful and inseparable wife. I was always loved and accepted by my family, but apart from them, I was rejected by everything and everyone, even by those I respected—mostly those inside the church. I understood rejection very well.

That helped me understand those who are rejected from this cruel world even better. As it was with my Lord, it was no different. The prophet Isaiah describes Jesus's situation in the world very well: "He is despised and rejected by men, a Man of sorrows and acquainted with grief. And we hid, as it were, our faces from Him; He was despised, and we did not esteem Him." (Isaiah 53:3)

Slowly, I understood that I could not be unsteady, soft, or smug to follow in Jesus's steps. I couldn't simply embrace a good idea. My sacrifice was necessary at every step. This "no" was my daily bread of bitterness. Besides my mother and Ester, was there anyone who could give me a single vote of confidence?

The "yes" came from God.

Just one word from the Bible held my spirits up, this time an excerpt from the letter of Apostle Paul to the church of Corinth: "But God has chosen the foolish things of the world to put to shame the wise, and God has chosen the weak things of the world to put to shame the things which are mighty; and the base things of the world and the things which are despised

God has chosen, and the things which are not, to bring to nothing the things that are,." (1 Corinthians 1:27-28)

Samuel Coutinho's words were so aggressive and humiliating that they even bothered the others who were present. There was a deadly silence in the room. Even the children were silent. The atmosphere became tense and awkward. Even as an unordained preacher, I was still very well respected by other assistants and workers. I would always bring a word of faith that often helped those in difficult moments when they talked to me.

Samuel himself perceived his intolerant behavior and changed the subject:

"Well then, let's pray. Let's speak to God."

Everyone went to their own corner. There were about 30 people at the meeting. I knelt down near a small table in the center of the room, and began my supplication. In fact, I had no idea how to start a prayer in so much pain. From the depths of my soul, I simply said:

"My Father...My Father..."

I was inwardly writhing in pain.

"My Father! My Father!"

It was different from anything else I had experienced. Simply uttering "my Father" in prayer makes sense, but in that state of my spirit, from the pit of my being, those two words took on a supernatural power. The comfort of heaven took over me.

"My Father!" I repeated, but in joy this time.

The comfort was such that I started smiling and then laughing out loud as I raised my voice and repeated the same terms.

"My Father! My Father!"

Everyone stopped praying and looked, wondering what was going on with me. It's hard to forget what happened or to explain the delight that took over me when I turned to the Holy Spirit. The Apostle Paul said it best, "Therefore I take pleasure in infirmities, in reproaches, in needs, in persecutions, in distresses, for Christ's sake. For when I am weak, then I am strong." (2 Corinthians 12:10)

The delight wasn't just some strong emotion or a momentary joy. It was far beyond that. The joy was not of the soul, but of the spirit. If it were of the soul, I would jump, dance, sing, and express a natural, physical happiness. But that was not the case. That moment marked me with an intense and awesome peace of spirit. The Spirit of God communicated with my spirit and completely soothed it. Amazing!

At this exact moment, as I recall and write what happened that evening, tears of joy fill my eyes.

I was touched by God Himself. Joseph was reprimanded by his father and brothers for having a heavenly dream: "Look, I have dreamed another dream. And this time, the sun, the moon, and the eleven stars bowed down to me." (Genesis 37:9)

The meeting that Friday ended with a completely new experience.

And so I continued as an evangelist, struggling to save more lives at the Bruni Méier Cinema.

A short time after that, we received some news. Since he knew the owners of the cinema chain, Soares had found another space for our work: the tiny Ridan Cinema in the

Abolição district, also in the northern zone of Rio de Janeiro. I stayed in Méier on Wednesdays, Fridays, and Sundays, and assisted in the outreach at Ridan the rest of the week. Even so, the work was slow. There were always few people—until one day Soares came with what seemed to be a fresh outlook.

"Edir, we managed to rent out Ridan only for us," he said, eyes gleaming. "It's all arranged with the owner. We will be establishing our church there."

We spent days working hard on cleaning the theater. We disinfected the bathrooms, washed the toilets and sinks, and scrubbed the floors and the seats. We were able to get the cinema into pristine condition. At the moment when he was just about to sign the papers and hand over the place, the owner backed out. The only way now was to go back to the services at the Méier Cinema.

In order to improve our meetings, I scheduled regular times every Saturday afternoon to preach at the pavilion in the main square of the district. The work was short and straightforward. We gathered the people, announced the power of Jesus, sang a traditional hymn, and cried out to God for miracles. I used to carry the sound equipment in my own car. A joyful song of faith, a prayer sung and played by a small organ, called for the people's attention:

If the troubles of this life are trying to pull you down,
Take hold of Jesus' hand and go.
If the sadness of this life is trying to break your heart,
Take hold of Jesus' hand and go.
Take hold of Jesus' hand, take hold of Jesus' hand,
For He, He will lift you up.

Don't fear, nor be afraid, just keep on straight ahead
Take hold of Jesus' hand and go.
If the journey seems too heavy, and makes you tired along the way,
Take hold of Jesus' hand and go.
Believing, rebuking, persisting and persevering
Take hold of Jesus' hand and go.
The Spirit of the Lord will always be clothing you,
Take hold of Jesus' hand and go.
Jesus Christ said in His word, He'd never leave you alone
hold on to God's hand and go.[11]

The people who walked past the pavilion knew something different was happening there. Even though I was only an evangelist, with no experience in spiritual deliverance, I dared to cast out evil spirits from the lives of those who watched me. People were curious. I would interview demons before forcing them to their knees and casting them out. A young man would always manifest strongly during those prayers, causing me to get dirty from head to toe.

The pavilion was filthy and had an unbearable stench of urine. Even so, I'd stand and give a teaching from the gospels.

---

11 *Se as águas do mar da vida quiserem te afogar/ Segura na mão de Deus e vai /Se as tristezas desta vida quiserem te sufocar/ Segura na mão de Deus e vai/ Segura na mão de Deus, segura na mão de Deus,/ pois ela, ela te sustentará/ Não temas segue adiante e não olhes para trás/ Segura na mão de Deus e vai / Se a jornada é pesada e te cansas da caminhada /Segura na mão de Deus e vai /Orando, jejuando, confiando e confessando /Segura na mão de Deus e vai /O Espírito do Senhor sempre te revestirá/ Segura na mão de Deus e vai / Jesus Cristo prometeu que jamais te deixará/ Segura na mão de Deus e vai.*

I always talked about salvation and prayed for those who wanted to accept Jesus. At the end, I handed out invitations to come to our meetings in the cinemas. Between five and 30 people started to faithfully attend my outdoor preaching. Every Saturday there was slight but noticeable progress.

Humble as it was, the work at the pavilion, scattered seeds that produce fruit to this day. I remember two widowed sisters who feared God and followed us to the meetings at the Méier Cinema, and always gave their tithe in fresh new bills sprinkled with a delicately scented powder on the envelope. The simpler the work, the greater is the power and the more God is relied upon. And the result, as expected, is a greater movement of the Holy Spirit. That is what I seek the most in the church these days: simplicity, the essence of God's work.

Every once in a while to this day, I meet people, usually elderly, who talk about how they were saved by one word they heard at that filthy, foul-smelling pavilion. Time has erased these messages from my memory, but they changed the lives of people I never saw again and will perhaps never see for the rest of my life. Souls won for the Kingdom of God. That pavilion produced faithful members and assistants, and even bishops of the Universal Church, many of whom have departed from this world. Men and women born from the Spirit that multiplied throughout the world.

There was as much salvation at that time as there is today. The reward? The privilege to serve Almighty God.

And it was at this pavilion that another character appeared who was indispensible for the growth of the Universal Church.

ALWAYS A SUSPECT

One day, I was upset as usual, and met one of the first participants of our meetings of faith at the Méier pavilion. Albino Silva da Costa, better known as Seu Albino, was a middle-class metal worker from the north zone of Rio. He was 53 at the time and tormented by serious problems in his family. His wife, Dona Maria, was also a born and bred Carioca—from Rio de Janeiro—and had been held captive by evil spirits since her youth.

She was always heavily medicated on tranquilizers, would faint suddenly for no reason, and wouldn't get out of bed for months because of chronic depression. She was 45 years old, but looked much older. Her daughters, students Alba and Rosalba, both felt empty and depressed. The family was suffering and turned to God for help at the pavilion meetings, as well as going the larger meetings in the Méier and Ridan Cinemas.

Seu Albino was in such agony, that day or night, he would rush to meet me for urgent help. Late one night, I got a desperate call because Dona Maria had suddenly fallen and fainted and had practically no vital signs. She seemed dead. I found her motionless in bed, while everyone looked at me and at her. I asked what had happened.

"Her mouth is busted open," Alba noticed in panic.

The scene was frightening.

I placed my hands on her head and prayed determinedly. No response. Dona Maria remained motionless. I prayed once more, and nothing happened.

"She's still stiff, she won't move," Seu Albino said.

At that moment, with the guidance of the Spirit of God, I remembered the prophet Elisha, who laid on top of a dead child and sent the Spirit to the child. "He went in, shut the door behind the two of them, and prayed to the Lord. And he went up and lay on the child, and put his mouth on his mouth, his eyes on his eyes, and his hands on his hands; and he stretched himself out on the child, and the flesh of the child became warm." (2 Kings 4:33-35)

"I am going to do something I've never done, but I believe in," I said spontaneously. "Excuse me, Seu Albino."

All of a sudden, I climbed on the bed and lay on top of Dona Maria. The devil could not resist, and immediately a demon manifested inside of her in a way I had never seen. I struggled hard through her deliverance; those were heavy-duty spirits. Soon afterwards Dona Maria regained consciousness and had been unaware of what had happened in the last few hours. That was but one of my battles in combat with hell as I started down the path as a servant of God. My second book of memoires will have more details of other powerful experiences I had in deliverance.

Seu Albino was so grateful for my help, that he became my partner for further work. One day, when we were relaxing and chatting after a service in Méier, I made a comment to him about an important step I had been dreaming of for my ministry.

"You see, Seu Albino, thanks to God, more and more people have gradually been seeking us out," I pondered, still trying to undo my tie. "You know, I should open a church. When we show up for the meetings, the theater is filthy and disgusting. I need to provide the best for these people."

"I am going to look for a place, Edir, I'll see what I can find," Seu Albino replied.

A few days later, he came up to me, excited.

"Edir, Edir! I saw an ad to rent an old funeral parlor here in Abolição. It seems to be a really good place. Would you like to come see it with me?"

When I entered the warehouse, my face lit up. I was imagining the future. I could see myself preaching on the altar in front of crowded wooden benches, miracles multiplying. Healings, deliverance, faith, revolt, salvation. Lives rescued from darkness. This was my place.

"Oh, Seu Albino," I sighed, eyeing every detail of the property that was still dirty and in disarray. "This is exactly what I want!"

"I can rent the hall, Edir. I've already spoken with the owner, we decided on the price, and everything is fine," he told me before revealing our next challenge. "But there's one problem. We don't have a guarantor. My house is mortgaged, otherwise I would do it right now."

The rent was high. 9,530 cruzeiros, which was the currency at the time. I didn't want him to haggle with the price and risk losing the property. I was determined to sign that contract. But how could I get a guarantor? Who would trust a young, 32-year-old preacher? Who would believe that from there, a church would rise up that would be able to pay its financial commitments on time and not be evicted? Who would believe in my dream? Who would believe in God's promise for my life?

I left the old funeral parlor with my thoughts spinning. Soon there was direction.

"I know. My mother, of course!" I told myself.

My great opportunity was about to happen. Once the lease was signed, I would start to dedicate myself full time to the new church. It was certain, at last, that I would quit my job. However, I would have to give up a reasonable salary and the stability of 16 years of public service. For humble families like mine, working as a public servant meant a guaranteed livelihood, free from the fear of unemployment.

I had started from the bottom. I had climbed step by step, from office boy up to head of the treasury. That career provided benefits, long vacations, and periodic pay-raises. After working at the lottery for 10 years, the State had awarded me a certificate of good services rendered. But as I had declared to God two years earlier, on the day of Viviane's birth, I would leave everything to preach the gospel. The punches of rage that I had let loose on that bed had brought about a revolution of faith.

My time had come.

I ran to ask my mother, Dona Geninha to be the guarantor. Alone with her, I explained how everything would happen. She just listened to me, agreeing with every word. I knew she would accept it right from the start. That's what mothers are for.

"All right, my son. I believe in you," she said. "I just want to make one request, dear. Take care not to lose your health insurance. Viviane needs it badly."

She was right. The job at the lottery ensured full medical benefits for me and my family, especially for little Viviane. She was only two years old and would have to undergo several surgeries on her mouth, on top of the treatment with expensive medication and full-time follow up with specialists. There was no way I could pay that bill. And without a salary, I wouldn't know what to do. But I had no doubts.

"Don't worry, Mom. God will help me," I assured her, thanking her for her vote of confidence with a tender kiss and a tight hug.

I really believed. The load of responsibilities on my shoulders weighed a ton. But I did not make many calculations. It was a snap decision, a lightning bolt of faith that led me to act without hesitation. The commitment to pay the rent didn't bother me. I was moved by an uncontainable confidence.

My mother guaranteed the lease contract with her only apartment as collateral, located on Glória Square. The agreement involved several obligations. A few days before signing, my brother-in-law, R. R. Soares, tried to persuade my mother to back out of the deal.

"Dona Geninha, don't do this, it's crazy. Your son can't afford to pay. You'll lose your apartment. Don't do this," Soares said, without an ounce of belief in me. "I've analyzed the contract in detail. If Edir defaults for just three months, they'll take away your home."

Soares did not believe in me, despite the fact that we had served in the work of God together. And he was not the only one. With the exception of Ester and my mother, many people were in doubt. Everyone thought I had a big label stuck on my forehead with the word "suspect," printed on it.

"No, Romildo. I will sign it. I believe in Edir," Dona Geninha declared.

My mother, in fact, did not back out. The lease contract was signed.

THE END OF THE DIVISION

The next step was to hand in my resignation at the lottery office. Again, I received more warnings of uncertainty and fear. Friends and relatives insisted I back off from the idea, arguing that I was trading a sure thing for something uncertain. They told me to be patient and wait until everything settled down. They said I shouldn't lose the security of a job since my small daughter depended on medical treatment that was paid for by the State health plan, and my own mother's apartment was being put on the line.

I closed my ears and made the decision on my own. Not even Ester knew the exact moment I handed in my resignation. I acted alone. The courage to do so did not come from within, but from the guidance and strength of the Holy Spirit. My word was a debt I had to pay. I reminded God of my promise and collected on His promise to me. It was pure faith, no emotion. Definite faith. God and me. I proved myself to the Lord God and He to me.

"Now is the time of decision. It's do or die!" I told the Holy Spirit in the few seconds before walking into the HR department and signing my letter of resignation.

There was not much to pray about. The action had been taken. More than ever, I was dependent on God. I was branded crazy, irresponsible, and inconsequential countless times after I left the lottery. People said I had put my future at risk. But I followed on, unabated in my faith.

Romildo Soares's opposing attitude would be a precursor of what was to happen in the future. It was not possible to be a co-partner in the leadership of the same church. His way of thinking was different from mine. Not that this leads me to believe that I was right or wrong, but simply that I had a different perspective. This is my faith and I am guided by it as I move ahead. A body cannot survive with two heads. There had to be a clear definition of goals and leadership. Intelligent faith requires definition.

We started the Universal Church together, but in the early 1980s, when I moved to the United States to preach the Word, hardship intensified. I was in New York, invited by a Portuguese family I had met in Abolição, of Rio de Janeiro. They used to attend our church and had recently moved back from the United States to Brazil, but wished to return to the U.S. again.

I soon saw an opportunity to spread the gospel to the world from one of the most influential metropolitan areas on the planet. I moved to New York with the financial support of the Portuguese father and daughters, who were totally fluent in English and knew the city very well. I planned to start an evangelistic work at a Veterans Association in Mount Vernon, half an hour north of New York City, but I had to return to Brazil in a hurry.

Soares's leadership, mainly his spiritual administration, was being questioned. The first problem was that he invited several pastors from other denominations to make up the board of preachers at the Universal Church. That was contrary to my principles of faith. Blending in old wine makes new wine sour. The so-called "imported pastors" brought with them a faith that was tainted by customs that did not match up with an intelligent faith. Secondly, because of basic inefficient management, the church began to lack the financial resources to honor its commitments. The administrative department employees would call me in New York to complain about not having the money to pay for rent and other expenses.

The third problem arose because his preaching became very personal, centering on the image of "Missionary R. R. Soares." He would only hold meetings if the assembly hall was full and was distancing himself from daily contact with the people by not counseling or attending to them. Everything that I would not do, started to happen in Rio de Janeiro.

I had no choice. I returned. Ester and the children had already returned to Brazil. I suspended the agreement to maintain my ministry in New York and packed my bags. It was no longer possible to share the church leadership with Soares. During the flight home, I thought about the talk I had with my brother-in-law a few days before the opening of the Universal Church, when we decided to share responsibilities.

"Soares, we will form a new church that transmits life and faith to people in an unprecedented manner. We will open the doors to a place that truly transforms people's lives," I told him with excitement. "You can be president, and I will be vice-president," I invited him.

"I was not born to be the tail, but the head. I was not born to be bossed about, but to be the boss," was his short, sharp response.

"It doesn't matter. I want to win souls," I replied.

Officially, the church minutes stated that Romildo Soares would be first secretary and I would be second secretary, but there was a tacit agreement that nothing would be done without consent from both parties. In hindsight, I recall that throughout my path of faith, I never thought about being the "boss" or "leader" of anything, let alone the owner of a TV network. My desire has always been to win souls. Winning souls over to the Kingdom of God was, and has always been, my goal. I couldn't care less about functions, positions, or the like. But, curiously enough, God placed on my shoulders responsibilities I had never imagined.

Upon arriving back in Rio de Janeiro, I sought out Soares so we could decide our future. In a respectful manner, we discussed recent events.

"Edir, I just want to grow quickly," he argued.

"But that won't work, Soares. The people are not happy with your meetings. These outsiders burden people down with constant preaching about sin. New pastors must grow and be raised up from among our own people, be formed by the Holy Spirit in the core of the church," I said.

"I don't agree, Edir," he insisted.

"So, we can't continue working together. Let's organize a vote to decide who will remain. If you win, I will submit with one condition: support from the church for the missionary work in New York. The same applies to you. If I win the vote, the church will provide you with support for your evangelistic work," I ended the conversation with Soares' agreement.

We summoned the 15 pastors for a special assembly to decide on the new leadership for the Universal Church. Voting took place on Saturday, June 7, 1980, in Abolição. Pastor Renato Maduro counted the votes. Bishop Paulo Roberto Guimarães and Carlos Rodrigues, a former bishop, also took part in the election. I had just celebrated Paulo's wedding before we rushed to vote.

Before voting began, we prayed. After that, I asked everyone to take stock of themselves, and consult the guidance of the Holy Spirit before casting their vote. After all, He was sent to us by the Lord Jesus to guide His servants.

One of the pastors collected the ballots. Renato Maduro read the results one by one:

"Pastor Macedo!" he announced emphatically, showing the vote to Soares.

"Missionary Soares," he read in a lower tone.

"Pastor Macedo! Pastor Macedo! Pastor Macedo!"

The end result was twelve votes for me and three against me. Soares, who was very disappointed, left the church and set off to carry out his religious work with the copyright for the books of evangelist T.L. Osborn.

After that, I temporarily canceled my plans to go to the United States. I remained with my companions to resume the construction of the Universal Church, which had been envisioned under the guidance of the Holy Spirit since the first preaching in the Méier pavilion.

THE DEAD IN THE FUNERAL PARLOR

Saturday morning, July 9, 1977. 7.428 Suburbana Avenue. It was a bustling morning in the Abolição district in Rio de Janeiro. There was intense movement at the old funeral parlor warehouse: cars parking, pedestrians walking up and down the sidewalks, buses dropping passengers off at nearby stops. It was the first service at the Universal Church of the Kingdom of God.

I woke up early, put on my best suit, organized the Bible, and left for the first gathering at my new ministry. I was euphoric and happy. God had answered my calls. The mass was about liberation, healing, and preaching the teachings to attain eternal life. With the stuffy heat in the hall, I was sweating under my hair and beard. I had not changed my appearance since I was young, even after becoming a preacher. I was myself, and that transparency in the way I acted called the attention of those who knew me.

A few days earlier, we had taken care of the minimum details to make the property functional. We painted the walls, scrubbed the floors, fixed the bathrooms—a full clean-up. The carpenters, hired at cost price, finished the last adjustments to the altar and the pulpit. The wooden benches, purchased in endless installments, were positioned to receive the new public.

Following our practice since the bandstand in the Méier Garden and the campaigns in the rented movie theaters in the region, we walked along the streets in Abolição and neighboring areas, handing out leaflets and invitations for the opening service.

On that Sunday, I meditated about Abraham, the father of faith, one of my most highly esteemed references in the Bible. He was an idealist, which I had always sought to be. And he abandoned everything in obedience to the voice of God. His call was heard by those who have spiritual ears: "The Lord had said to Abraham, 'Go from your country, your people and your father's household to the land I will show you. I will make you into a great nation, and I will bless you; I will make your name great, and you will be a blessing'" (Genesis 12:1-2).

The patriarch was promised he would be the father, the point or origin, of an entire nation when, married to infertile Sarah, he could not even bear a child. And when fears and doubts befell Abraham, God encouraged him with an image that is available to this day to those who have spiritual eyes. "He took him outside and said, 'Look up at the sky and count the stars—if indeed you can count them.' Then he said to him, 'So shall your offspring be'" (Genesis 15:5).

My history follows the example of Abraham. How many times, as an evangelist and even before that, after my new birth in Rio de Janeiro, I would open my house window and look up to observe the same stars Abraham saw. They remain firm in the heavens, not just to be admired, but above all, to witness how the word of Abraham's God is as true today as it was in the past.

I had taken a risk by abandoning everything to follow the voice of God. I struggled to be a missionary as Abraham had done. To this day, I envision this idealist saga. Visionaries have new ideas and unveil new horizons. Modern philosophy itself, in parts of its doctrines, defines idealism as a theory according to which the material world can only be fully comprehended from its spiritual truth. Idealists use their capacity of intelligence to understand.

From the Universal Church opening on that Saturday to this day, that is and will always be my fate, my greatest legacy. Like Abraham, we must use intelligent faith discerned in our minds to attain God's promises. It was such idealism, guided by the Holy Ghost, that started to attract a surprising crowd to the old funeral parlor hall week after week. It was not long before the church became too small for the number of believers.

Despite all the humiliation I had endured, I was still linked to the Eternal Path Crusade, led by Samuel Coutinho and Romildo Soares. Coutinho was still president, but the two of them already showed signs of dissidence. I was concerned about wasting all the effort spent on the funeral parlor building on a possible fight in the future, and in the official document, I registered the institution as the Church of Blessing. But for me and the members at that time, we were already living the first days of the Universal Church.

On a Friday night, Coutinho appeared suddenly at the Church with three assistants.

"Edir, this Church is mine! You can't drive it alone!" he shouted at me.

Although his name was registered in the founding statute, Soares was absent during that period. He was involved in personal businesses and missionary work in São Paulo. He did not even know that Coutinho had invaded the old funeral parlor to take the Church from us. It was the last straw.

"Coutinho, you only want the Church because it is full. This church belongs to the people, to God. You can't take it from us," I replied, while workers and evangelists crowded around, angry at the offensive posture of the president of the Eternal Path Crusade.

There was threat of a commotion until Coutinho and his partners left the Abolição district. That was our definite and official break-up. The last time I saw Samuel Coutinho was two years later, in the vicinity of the Metropolitana Radio in Ihnaúma. As soon as the Universal Church started to rent out time slots from the Metropolitana, attracting crowds, other denominations ran to copy us.

"You took that Church from me, Edir!" he shouted when he saw me in the corridor of the station, pushing me with his hands and threatening to physically assault me.

The funeral parlor, in fact, was a landmark. It was there that I was consecrated pastor on my 33rd birthday, February 18, 1978. Seu Albino presented me with the suit I wore for that special ceremony.

At the end of the service, a historic, black-and-white photograph was taken for my consecration, which recorded

Ester, me, and my daughters beside Seu Albino's family. It was an unforgettable moment, just like when the Holy Ghost inspired us to transmit a clear, straightforward message on the doors and altars of the Church.

"Why not place an inscription on the front of the building and the altar wall to announce our belief?" I asked some workers gathered with me inside the funeral parlor.

"Jesus Christ is the Lord" became a symbolic phrase for our movement of faith. I thought of how I used to be disappointed by seeing the arrogance of man in several congregations and religious institutions. Many of those places displayed a sign on the temple door reading, "So-and-so Church built for the glory of God by missionary so-and-so." One glory for God and another one for the founder. That made me sick. And that is what I was forced to swallow at the New Life and Eternal Path Crusade Churches.

I decided to do it differently. No Bishop Macedo or any other founding bishop in evidence. At the Universal Church, only Jesus Christ is the Lord. That does not mean a lack of acknowledgement to those who helped us at the onset of this journey. I have respectful and nostalgic recollections of those men and women of substance. I always ask pastors to give special attention to our "house silverware."

That is, the members or workers who contributed in some way, even in the simplest form, to make the church what it is today. From those who painted the walls, scrubbed the bathrooms, and donated fans, curtains, and flower trinkets, to those who fitted the wooden benches, nailed the first letters of the inscription to the altar, and prayed and served the people: each one added a little brick in the work of God.

We know about the hand of God all over this work, and for that reason only, we are what we are today. But it is essential to acknowledge the effort of those who sheltered us in our first steps. That is why I approved the idea for a team of documentary makers, who were making a special program about the Temple of Solomon, to invite some of our first collaborators to see this project, unheard of in the world. Seu Albino was one of the chosen. The journalists would later tell me about his gratitude and joy when he saw the temple close up, at the same time recalling the day, more than three decades ago, that he found the small funeral parlor hall to be leased.

I have selected a short excerpt from the reporter's recordings with Seu Albino on the grounds of the Temple of Solomon in Brás, São Paulo.

Reporter: Seu Albino, 89, one of the Universal Church pioneers, has come from Rio de Janeiro, his home town, especially to see the construction work of the Temple of Solomon. At our invitation, he is one of the first believers to see the place. What do you think, Seu Albino? Exciting?

Albino: It's...It's really out of this world...Wow, the greatness of the place is impressive. (Silence, contemplating the 30-meters-high side columns.)

Albino: Did you go to Israel for inspiration?

(He asks the architect responsible for the construction as he looks at a model replica of the temple.)

Architect: Yes. We went there several times. I, for one. went six times, but unfortunately, the temple no longer exists. What exists today is the Wailing Wall and some stones. Actually, we will be using for the Temple of Solomon the same stones that were used in the temple there...The stones of Hebron in Israel. Bishop Edir Macedo's idea to bring a piece of Israel over here so that when people touch the walls, they can pray. A piece of Israel in Brazil...

Albino: It's really impressive...Will it be the biggest church in Brazil?

Architect: I think so. In capacity, it's not bigger than the Del Castilho Cathedral, on the avenue where you helped start the Universal Church, but in physical space and importance it is unique. Especially because the Temple of Solomon no longer exists, only the Wailing Wall. We will be making the environment as close as possible to the original temple, but here it will be acclimatized and lighted. The air conditioner ducts and lighting will not be visible, but we will have it all.

Albino: Wow, it will look beautiful! And when will it be finished?

Architect: It is forecast for May 2014, but it might be finished earlier.

Reporter: How many memories, Seu Albino? The beginning was very different, right?

Albino: I would do it all over again, I get great satisfaction...I didn't imagine the Church would grow so much, no way. God is really great.

(With tearful eyes, touching the cement walls, walking with difficulty through the temple construction works.)

The full dialogue, of course, will be shown on Record Network in this documentary prepared for the period of inauguration. But I leave here my special and true thanks to Seu Albino and so many anonymous people who helped us. I am sure that their greater reward is reserved in the heavens.

What is most striking from that period is to look at the past and understand the symbolic reasons that the Universal Church came into existence, in a funeral parlor. It is impossible not to recall the psalmist's reflection on God's vocation: "He raises the poor from the dust and lifts the needy from the ash heap; he seats them with princes, with the princes of his people" (Psalm 113:7-8).

How many dead in spirit were revived at the same place that cadavers were prepared for their wake and burial? As with Ezekiel's prophecy in the Valley of Dry Bones, the same happened to me and the Universal Church in that previous room for the dead. "This is what the Sovereign Lord says to these bones: I will make breath enter you, and you will come to life" (Ezekiel 37:5).

Bishop Renato Maduro, one of our first workers, was another dry bone gathered by the power of God. He arrived at the Universal Church from inside the funeral parlor. He was a man who was dead from an uncontrollable and devastating addiction to drugs. The first time I saw him was entering the church, and as a brother, I followed him closely, observing his liberation and growth as a man of God. His death on December 12, 2010, made me recall this. As with him in the funeral parlor, God rescued thousands of people in that simple, remote warehouse. Maduro dedicated his life to recover suffering souls.

He suffered, struggled, groaned, and sacrificed his youth. He won. Maduro died with a smile. Where did his soul go?

That moment, during the resurrection of the "dead" in the funeral parlor, was the beginning of the Universal Church we know today. It was all minuscule, something very small indeed next to so many extraordinary situations we would live through. Innumerable struggles would place us between life and death, but would give us countless, uncommon trophies. Hundreds of countries, thousands of pastors, millions of workers and loyal members. A church that pulsates faith and life. Souls won over to the Kingdom of God.

My all

I have set aside some more untold spiritual secrets from my journey for my next book, but I finish this one with one question: what is the most important thing in this world after finding God, receiving the Holy Spirit, and wholly surrendering my life on the altar? Nothing else is of value. Things lose their meaning. The values many fight to the death for are of no importance to me—success, money, position, status, recognition, power. I've found such a tremendous possession that everything else on this earth has become worthless.

One day during an interview, a reporter asked about my secret to accomplishing so much. Expecting a profound philosophical answer, he was surprised by what I said.

"Giving. Simply giving," I replied plainly.

So simple, so mundane, so common, but extremely difficult to put into practice, especially for those who have their hearts set on the world's standards. My reply is no different than the promise the Lord Jesus made, "Give, and it will be given to you..." (Luke 6:38) Since the first days in my struggle to be converted, I relearn this lesson every moment I live. It's a lesson that is made new with every dawn—the more we give, the more we receive. There is no other secret.

My life is an example of this simplistic, revolutionary concept for success. I hold responsibilities I would never have imagined in the past, as a result of the time I dedicated to God as an evangelist in the cinemas and squares in Rio de Janeiro, where I was forced to announce the preaching of pastors and missionaries with inflated egos. I dedicated 24 hours of my routine to the church, and to recording messages of faith for broadcast companies who only exist to spread the Word of God. The work has become so strong, with a huge presence and widespread movements on so many fronts all over the planet, that many can't imagine that Ester and I live extremely simple lives, but we do.

This is the life of a pastor of the Universal Church. Like John the Baptist, a solitary man of the desert, who fed on locusts and wild honey and possessed nothing. Better still, he had nothing and everything at the same time, because he remained faithful to God, preaching repentance and preparing for the arrival of the Lord Jesus, the Savior of mankind.

This is how I lead my day-to-day life: "stuck" in the church in full service to our God. Many even insist that I enjoy the delights and pleasures of the world, but that doesn't tempt me. It doesn't satisfy my spirit. I have everything, but

I have nothing. The Universal Church, Record Network, my wife, my children, my life. After all, nothing belongs to me. It all seems to be mine, but actually, it's only borrowed.

Now I can understand a prayer I made on Thursday evening, February 15, 2010, in Santo Amaro, São Paulo. Hours earlier, I had meditated about Manasseh, King of Judah, the royal commander in an era of massive crime, disgrace, and perversity. Manasseh even sacrificed his own sons to demons in an act of defiance to God. Even so, in his moment of deepest shame, when he repented and humbled himself, the Lord heard his voice and restored him. How great was His mercy.

If Manasseh was rescued, there is no human being who cannot be rescued as well. There is no impossible situation for God. This is the prayer I prayed:

Dear Father, I am a father, I am a son, I am a brother, I am a husband. I feel, my Lord, the pains of humiliation Your people feel because we know what it's like. Hear the groans of Your people. I say groans because sometimes there are no words to express their pain.

Oh, my Father, You heard Manasseh's prayer, who was perverse, cruel, immoral, and hostile. He attacked You, challenged You, and made fun of You. He did all kinds of evil that we have never done. Even so, when he humbled himself, You descended from Your place and answered his plea.

Look at each of us now. What have we done? How have we displeased You? Whatever it may be, Lord, we are not perfect, but we are not as he was. We are not, but we humbly come before You now my Lord, as Manasseh humbled himself, in the dust.

For we, Your servants, pastors, bishops, also carry groans, shame, and pain within our souls. And there are times we have to strengthen people when we ourselves are weak, turned frail by circumstances.

Listen, my Father, listen from heaven and answer Your people because You are not a God of wood and stone. You are truly God. Spirit and Truth. Under Your Word, we place our lives on the altar. We unite our voices, our cries, our faith. Pastors, assistants, the people, everyone, in one spirit, with one cry, calling on one Lord—the God of Abraham, of Isaac, of Israel.

Oh, come at this moment, my Father, to manifest Your glory and bring the answer we have been seeking for years. We have no one else to turn to. There is pain in our heart, the pain of humiliation, my Father.

My Lord, all that we, Your servants, want is to please You, to serve You. We do not care about the filth, the waste of this world. We do not care about any of this gsrbage!

We have nothing to lose because we have nothing! What we have is our life on Your altar!

Come to take our pains, our groans. We have no one else to cry out to, we have no one to turn to. We only have You, Jesus. Oh, come my Friend, my Father... Come upon us and take the shame from our hearts.

Take it, my Father. Take it all...

(crying)

...because we do not know what else to do, my Lord.

(crying)

We no longer know how to act. Come, my Lord. Yes, Lord, take our life once and for all if you will, my Father. I have no pleasure in living this way, my Lord, in endless humiliation. There is no pleasure, my Father... If You were to take me now, what a favor You would be doing.

I no longer know what to say. I only carry this pain inside me. (crying)

We are under Your word, my Lord. When I get up from the floor, I want to be absolutely sure You have heard and replied. I want to see, my Lord, Your glory in the face of Your people. I want to see Your people smiling, with shining eyes. I want to see joy in the hearts of Your people.

Oh, Holy Spirit, we put our lives before You. Judge our case, judge Yourself as You judged Hannah, as you judged the cases of Your servants in the past. In the name of Jesus I ask of You, I plead to You that the sick and the weak rise from their beds. That those with cancer, the paralytics, the blind, the deaf be healed.

Be free now, those who hear me at this moment, and may it be known that the God of Abraham, Isaac, and Israel is our God.

He hears our plea, it is the Lord of the Universal Church of the Kingdom of God. It is the God that has carried and sustained this work.

Receive the Holy Spirit, you who need your thirst quenched. Be baptized in the Holy Spirit, you who do not fully understand, but who want to find Jesus.

He is manifesting Himself to you right now. Find the Jesus we have been preaching, encounter the God we have been proclaiming. Receive now, at this moment, the living God, the God of Abraham, of Isaac, the God of Israel, in the name of the Lord Jesus.

This prayer is my life at the altar.

As I told God, I have nothing to lose.

Though I happen to be the spiritual leader of a church that is currently present in more than 200 countries, and though I am also the owner of the second largest television broadcasting company in Brazil, reaching 200 million viewers worldwide, as well as the owner of newspapers, radio broadcasting companies, and many other projects and activities, and though I have a wonderful, exemplary wife and children who fill me with satisfaction, none of that comes even close to my greatest possession. Nothing is worth more than my close relationship with God.

My God, the Holy Spirit, dwells within me as the most honored one in my being. He is my most valuable treasure. My happiness. My comfort. My Lord in battle. My hope. My truth. My salvation.

My all.